The art of God
and the religions of Art

The art of God
and the religions of Art

David Thistlethwaite

WIPF & STOCK · Eugene, Oregon

Wipf and Stock Publishers
199 W 8th Ave, Suite 3
Eugene, OR 97401

A John Hick Reader
By Hick, John and Badham, Paul
Copyright©1990 Palgrave Macmillan
ISBN 13: 978-1-61097-562-9
Publication date 7/1/2011
Previously published by Trinity Press International, 1990

Now when Paul was waiting for them at Athens, his spirit was provoked within him as he saw that the city was full of idols.

Acts of the Apostles 17:16

It appears to me that pictures have been over-valued; held up by a blind admiration as ideal things, and almost as standards by which nature is to be judged rather than the reverse; and this false estimate has been sanctioned by the extravagant epithets that have been applied to painters, as 'the divine', 'the inspired', and so forth. Yet in reality, what are the most sublime productions of the pencil but selections of some of the forms of nature, and copies of a few of her evanescent effects; and this is the result, not of inspiration, but of long and patient study, under the direction of much good sense.

John Constable, *Discourses*.

Contents

Foreword

The song that David Thistlethwaite is singing here has immense presence, because the voice of the singer is singing singularly, like a shrill sound at a wedding banquet. What is more remarkable, it is the Bride herself who sings to her Husband, who pours forth her heart, her yearning for her Husband. I behold hope in these pages, hope in the twilight of this epoch and to the dry bones, that the breath of the Spirit breathes to give life. I more than applaud and welcome; I say, this is food indeed.

Samuel Taylor Coleridge put it another way:

It is an ancient Mariner
And he stoppeth one of three.
'By thy long grey beard and glittering eye,
Now wherefore stopp'st thou me?

The Bridegroom's doors are opened wide,
And I am next of kin;
The guests are met, the feast is set:
Mayst hear the merry din.'

He holds him with his skinny hand,
'There was a ship,' quoth he.
'Hold off! unhand me, grey-beard loon!'
Eftsoons his hand dropt he.

He holds him with his glittering eye—
The Wedding-Guest stood still,
And listens like a three years' child:
The Mariner hath his will.

The Wedding-Guest sat on a stone:
He cannot choose but hear;
And thus spake on that ancient man,
The bright-eyed Mariner.

The point to catch your elbow, is not agreement, it is provocation – for goodness' sake be provoked, be stirred, debate – here, dear friends, there is much to debate, for there is much at stake.

> To this John replied, 'A man can receive only what is given him from heaven. You yourselves can testify that I said "I am not the Christ but am sent ahead of him." The bride belongs to the bridegroom. The friend who attends the bridegroom waits and listens for him, and is full of joy when he hears the bridegroom's voice. That joy is mine, and it is now complete. He must become greater; I must become less.' (John 3:27–30, NIV)

We are in an age before the end, and I do hear and see, as I have said, 'hope'; because our hope is in the Bridegroom, in Jesus. What is here announced, what is here before you to be announced, will challenge; for it is about more of him and less of us. We are in the days of John again, this is a voice of one calling in the desert, 'Make straight the way of the Lord.' Our question is, what on earth will we do with this?

Dry is the land and in need of such provocation; for the question of creation and creativity is at the very pith of our being. But why, we may add, is there any creation at all? God does not need it, yet paradoxically it exists – perhaps we can answer this question with another – why do paintings and symphonies exist? We do not need either – not the way we need food and drink. In a similar way, the creation exists as a work of art in which God takes pleasure and through which he gives pleasure. God is like the artist who loves to create and who delights in what is made.

'Something of the why of creation is revealed by the Nature of God', writes Charles Pinnock in *Trinitarian Creation, Flame of Love*. So, to explore God's form of who he is and how he works, of how he makes things, can tell us about ourselves for we are gloriously made in his image.

In 1955 David Jones posed some very serious questions in an essay called 'Art as Sacrament'. It was a cry from the heart; how are we to reconcile man-the-artist, man the sign-maker or sacrament-maker with the world in which we live today? He spoke about a divorce, in our civilization, an agreed separation; but his article was, in his own words, nothing beyond an enquiry. His questions were a gauntlet thrown down to image bearers and image-makers – so let's listen and be challenged and ponder David Thistlethwaite's song in *The art of God*, for he has laid hold of a very serious question.

Richard Kenton Webb
Cirencester
June, 1998

Acknowledgements

Until I had written a book I never understood how indebted an author feels. At the beginning I thought it was to be 'all my own work'; by the end I wondered if any of it was! So here, without mentioning any of the specific intellectual ingredients of the book, I would like to honour those who have helped me so much.

First of all I must mention my school art teacher Tom Griffiths, and my history teachers Robin Reeve and Ted Maidment, for whom thinking was a way of life; later, there was that eminent Cambridge teacher Michael Jaffé, who made us spend real time with real works of art and who never failed to demand the best. Colleagues, friends and employers, at Agnew's the art dealers also generously taught their skills in looking at paintings. Back at Cambridge, I was helped by art theory and aesthetics teachers Duncan Robinson and Michael Tanner. Their tolerant and hands-off research supervision permitted germs of ideas to grow. Several friendships also contributed much to my education; particularly I remember grate - fully the patient encouragement of Michael Beddow and David Habak - kuk, who did so much to widen my horizons of literature and art. The first to open theological doors for me was the then Cambridge preacher Dennis Lennon, who made an intellectual adventure of faithfulness to Scripture and whose speaking exemplified the value of creativity for truth. Professor James Torrance gave vital encouragement at a critical time, and my friendship with his son Alan and pupils Stephen May and Jeremy Begbie helped keep me on track. This more or less accounts for the period of gestation.

Subsequently I have benefited from some great spiritual teachers, particularly two Pentecostal men of God, Trevor Davey and Brian Niblock, and a father in God, the late Richard Conner, who with his wife Joyce pioneered a practical theology of marriage with deep impli - cations for other aspects of creation, such as art. The late Brian Myers, another pioneer in his field, introduced me to the tricky subject of demonology and was of great personal help in this area. Next I should mention Oliver Barclay, whose passion to see Christian truth applied to every area of professional and intellectual life brought me into UCCF (the Universities and Colleges Christian Fellowship organization), through which I had many mind-stretching encounters on the theme of Christian faith and work – with scientists, farmers, vets, architects, engineers, etc. as well as with other more 'normal' people like historians, and artists – and which gave me unlimited opportunities to write.

Finally, for enabling the book to get written at all, I must thank Pieter Kwant of Paternoster Publishing for suggesting it and Peter Cousins, who as editor proved himself perhaps the one person whose enthusiasm and whose breadth of artistic, theological and literary interests could have got the book out of me. I have greatly benefited from the comments of readers Jeremy Begbie, Paul Joannides and Norman Housely, and from Elria Kwant's thoughtful and painstaking work on the manuscript.

Less publicly, but not less important I imagine, there is a secret work undertaken by those who have prayed for the book, and for our family during the writing, and who may justly take credit for any spiritual strengths it has. Our two children have been surprisingly constant in their encouragement and have taught me so much by their own creativity. The person whose contribution I cannot fairly assess, because her care and encouragement are so all-pervasive, is my wife Ali, but to go into all that she has done for me by friendship, help and example, would require a separate book.

My main *intellectual debts* will be evident during the course of the book, especially in the personal account which appears in Chapter 5, and also from the notes and Bibliography. As will be seen, for me the works of some writers (and others I have not been able to mention) have done more than satisfy an intellectual quest; at certain stages, it has felt like being given one's life back.

Preface

You have a book in your hands which is probably a bit different from
what you expect. The title, 'the art of God and the religions of Art',
exactly describes it; but it introduces some ideas which may well need a
little elbow room, if they are to fit into one's normal thinking about art.
'Are you writing about religious art?' people have often said to me. 'Yes,
but there are not many religious paintings illustrated in the book, and
icons are mentioned only once. No, I am not writing about religious, or
Christian art on the one hand, and secular, uncommitted art on the other.
I do not see the division like that.' By this time, I fear to have lost them.
But I really do not like those categories. In any case, most people who
love art, love art. We need to start somewhere else.

This book is about religion, not as something religiously-minded
people can opt into, but as something we are in, whether we like it or
not. It is about the place of art in that religious dynamic of life. But the
word 'religion' is not always used positively in the book. Religion, as
most of us know, can be a pretty exhausting and destructive business, with
very few positive benefits, though with undeniable attractions. We will
be trying to understand art's involvement with religion in that sense. This
will be seen throughout history, but particularly in that place and time
which most thinks it has escaped from religion: the secular West in the
twentieth century.

In talking about 'the art of God', however, we will be trying to
understand art and religion in quite a different sense. When we think of
art, we will be thinking of something that is simply there, as trees, and
birds, and birds' nests are, in the Creation. Of course human art is different
from birds' nests, because we are humans, with different capacities and
roles. But there is an art which is simply there. At the higher levels, it
may, or may not, be 'religious' in subject matter. But what makes it art
goes behind that, to the way we were made.

And when we talk about the 'religion' that this art was made to be
involved in, it is the least 'religious' kind of religion we know. 'The art
of God' is not an art we strain after, with all the anxiety that religion
usually produces. It is an art which we were intended to be *included into*.
This may be, and at its best is, an art 'towards' God. But essentially it is

an art *from* God, not just to be enjoyed like meals, and sunshine, and other material gifts in creation, but from God personally, as a gift in the doing of it.

This may, admittedly, take you further than you were planning to go. Willingness to travel in this direction will depend at least partly on our contentment with art at present. Some will take art very much as it comes, and have no questions about the present direction of art. Many will never have experienced the need to heal, and sometimes to forgive, the relationship between church and art. But for those who want practically to get into an art cleared of some of the hindrances of the past, hindrances which even the revolutionary freedoms of the twentieth century have left behind, these unexpected structures of thinking may be helpful.

I have enjoyed writing this book. Doing so has given me confidence that my own lifelong desire to integrate religion and art is possible without compromise to either; provided one integrates the right bits of both. As for the parts of religion and art that should be at enmity, that is a story that will also be found in this book – and I am happy for that battle to continue.

Leicester
May 1998

PART I

ART AS CREATED

We begin with a look at art as it was created to be. This is an art, of course, for which there is absolutely no physical evidence; which has not, of course, stopped it being extensively written on.

The point of our imaginary reconstruction, particularly using the Bible, is simple. When you or I use the word 'Art', we are conditioned by its history; particularly during the last three hundred years, when art has been a separate category of objects we look at in art galleries. I happen to like art galleries – but the mentality behind this conception of art is different from the thinking that produced most of the art in the first place. The 'gallery' concept of art is, ironically, not the most helpful way of filling galleries. It has been widely agreed that this viewer-oriented idea of art has cut art off from its roots. But what are its roots?

'Creation' is a concept we normally apply, if we apply it at all, to things other than man-made. What humans get up to, after they are made, is thought of as their own invention, once God's handiwork is finished. But there are certain structures of life that seem to come with the physical creation; such as the way the original man and woman were supposed to live with each other. There is a 'where to live' aspect of creation, but there is also a 'how to live'.

I do not find it far-fetched to think of art as one of the 'institutions' of Creation, that flow directly from our nature and situation in the world. And like all such institutions, it is open to acceptance, alteration, or even abuse.

Chapter One

Art in Creation

'Creation' – a dull word, a seized word, a bullied word, a hackneyed word: but it need not be, once you get the hang of it. 'Creation' is something to look for, a way of seeing the world. It also refreshes art. It helps us see what art is, in itself; it helps us see the world that art is supposed to see. 'Creation' is more than an off-the-shelf theological concept: it is our history, written into our bones, if not our textbooks. It is our identity; it is our destiny.

What is Creation?

Today is the day of creation. Today thousands, or is it millions, of people draw breath for the first time. Countless animals, bugs and plants have their first hours of life. And within each created being are capacities waiting to be discovered: to feed, to reproduce, to enjoy in some fashion, and to work. Each creature will change the world before it dies. And the human creatures, makers, meddlers and menders, will change the world very much. This is creation, an explosion of activity, and it starts today.

Does this view of creation seem surprising? We are so used to peering at it down a long time-tunnel that we forget how artificial, and how misleading, this telescopic image is. A time-tunnel, however good our vision, implies a loss of focus. 'Creation' can safely occupy the romantic distance, and our imaginations, strengthened by this or that dogma, can fill it out as they please. But Creation is what *is*, all around us, the extraordinary, super-ordinary and just plain ordinary, the unstoppable, teeming life of the planet, the worlds and stars.

It is true that Adam's history book had fewer pages in it than ours. The world he inherited had not been complicated by the mistakes of forbears. The air was fresher! But in important respects, Creation was neither older nor younger than it is for us. Our own trees, animals and people are pretty well brand new. Our mountains are antiques, just as his were, and as they should be. Like us, Adam had only today and yesterday. His yesterday was unchangeable, just as ours is. His today was open, but conditioned by yesterday, just as ours is. For practical purposes, we have no more and no less time than he did: we all have today; and creation consists in what we can do with today. We start from a different point to him, so our options are different. There are things he could do that we cannot do (like hunt for the Dodo), but in some ways our options are very much greater. There are people and creatures born after Adam of whose existence he was, so to speak, deprived. But undoubtedly he had sufficient creation to occupy a lifetime, and so do we.

The value of looking at the concept of 'Creation' as referring to the world around us, rather than thinking of it as some faded map of the real reality in the past, is that it helps us realize how much the idea has become encrusted with romantic and pseudo-biblical associations. The 'Adam' of our picture books does not love the smell of engine oil or the noise of Formula One, dig tunnels or build motorways. His innocence we secretly associate with inactivity. He gardens, but scarcely to disturb what is there. He has no schemes. In short, Eden is a hotel, not a home he has made his own.

Having got a false view of Creation, we then use our 'in the beginning' to define for us what life is now, rather than looking at what we have got. It is true that we feel impelled by the very fallibility of the world to establish a standard of perfection: but there is something more than horticultural perfection – there is who we are, every dimension of us, political, technical, creative, and where we are going. Creation is not the pre-evolved; 'Creation' is who we are, apart from our sin. To get a sense of Creation, we need to immerse ourselves in the happenings of today.

(*Today, in Leicester where I live, an artist has been out early, and has painted all yesterday's drabness with colour. Stripes of orange-yellow cross the road, and run up the sides of the trees. Next to them are violets, blues and greens, shimmering as shadows. Touches of red dot the chimneys, where yesterday there was grey-brown. Fiery blue (yes, fire is blue) fills the sky. Why had this been done? No Council employed him. No government on earth could afford him. Little thanks is given. Yet the vitality that this crisp, clear colour infuses to three hundred thousand Leicester lives will impart cheerfulness, neighbourliness, and energy. Doctors don't need to bottle it; it's there! And I'm off painting!*)

Obstacles to 'seeing' Creation

Let me tell you what we are aiming at in talking about Creation: and then we will see how much is in the way. We need to arrive at a sense that the things in the world matter; people, objects. Without that, art as it has been given to us is frustrated. If I mention the name 'Cézanne', for example, we will think of someone to whom things in the world – apples, still-life objects, landscape, light – mattered intensely. The assumption that seen things matter drew out of him a labour that still engages us in his paintings; we are drawn in as participants in his restless quest to realize, to give its due, to what is there. And he, though not the most vocal of

Catholic believers, seems to have acknowledged the source of things
mattering, in the Creator God: 'lines parallel to the horizon give depth',
he instructs a young painter, 'whether it is a section of nature or, if you
prefer, of the show which the *Pater Omnipotens Aeterne Deus* spreads out
before our eyes'.[1] Sometimes Cézanne expressed his relationship to nature
in the subjective language of his time; but though he talked about his
'sensations', it was nature to which he constantly referred his pupil's
attention.

The understanding of things mattering that we are after is of a particular
kind. If things matter because God made them and cares for them, then
they matter in a virtual infinity of aspects; and they also matter as a whole.
As moderns, we characteristically substitute for this general sense that
things matter for themselves (their own right to be there, and to tell us
their story, which is historically one of the main stimuli of art), the
utilitarian idea that things can only matter for some 'useful purpose'.
Cézanne, on this understanding, was not interested in apples as apples,
but because they were spherical, or a bit more difficult to paint than
spherical! If we are interested in them, it is as food, or as commodities.
Nothing is fully itself; everything has to be anatomized into some useful
constituents. The end result is that in our perceptions we become the
prisoners of our concepts. When we look at fellow human beings, it is
becoming increasingly hard to see them as whole persons, and not to
superimpose a vision in which they are an impersonal assemblage of
floating code called genes, or the containers of an unreliable mechanism
called a psyche. The person, who can be addressed as a whole, is in danger
of falling apart. If, on the other hand, we see things through the eyes of
Creation, everything re-integrates. We see things (and people) not as the
projections of our own concepts, but as truly other to ourselves, because
in some sense they are owned and vouched for by a personal God. And
that is where encounter with them starts to get exciting.

That, as I say, is where in general we want to get to by studying Creation.
In particular, we will be trying to get at the created nature of art, as
something that is a given feature of the world, outside ourselves and, if it is
going to work, outside our tampering. But I am not sure we can 'see'
Creation, get there, really get there so that we can feel its truth, straightaway,
simply because of where we are as late twentieth-century people. I am one
who would happily take the Bible, open its first few chapters, and ask what
God has to show us about art; but that I can do so, and regard that as a
rational thing to do, is only because a certain amount of debris has been
cleared away first. We cannot shovel debris at length, but we can at least
attend briefly to some of the unquiet voices which will otherwise rob us of
the experience of Creation which we ought to have.

---

[1] *Cézanne Letters*, ed. John Rewald, p. 301. However, there is a notable absence
of other references to God in respect of nature.

The goodness that is not there (and the 'middle ground' of art)

If we are going to try to see and feel 'Creation', the first unquiet voice any artist will have to deal with is that the goodness of creation so often disappoints. The great nineteenth-century critic, John Ruskin, eager in his youth to preach God through nature, me t his moment of disillusion-ment when he found a dead sheep in a ditch! His contemporary Tennyson marked the shock of the betrayed romantic in the oft-quoted phrase 'nature red in tooth and claw'. Latterly, Bishop Lesslie Newbig in has echoed this in a response to the new romanticism of deep ecology: 'To make nature our ultimate is to be delivered to death. Nature's smile can be charming, but her teeth are cruel.'[2] The sense that nature is never quite what we want it to be has not infrequently resulted in such despair, that we cease appreciating it for what it is.

The pain of nature's not living up to its promise, at least its aesthetic promise, is perfectly real. But before one responds by quickly swallowing a theological pain-killer, in the shape of the doctrine of the Fall – by which we understand that nature is not what it should be, because of humanity's rebellion – it is worth dwelling on the pain itself. For it is the very fact that nature painfully points two ways that is as much evidence for a benign Creation as against it. And it is here that art, counselled by theology, is very potent. Nature may be resistant to concepts, and ready to buck and kick against such an encompassing concept as Romanticism, but when we know what to look for, it is eager to show the glory that remains. The doctrine of 'the Fall' need not be taken as a palliative, to numb pain by retreat into theory, but can open us out to look for all the dimensions of Creation, without being too programmatic about what we shall find.

One of the earliest landscape artists to perhaps deliberately express the ambivalent signals of nature was the seventeenth-century Dutch painter, Jacob Ruisdael. Ruisdael's peculiar gift was to be able to be moved, and to move us, by the whole landscape in all its moods – the poetry of stormcloud and wind, the sense of hope in distant bursts of light – and yet also to see the whole condition of the shadowed land as a God–given symbol, of a Creation which has fallen away from its 'sun'.[3] Shadow conveys the sense of a created structure which does not change, but whose full colour and radiance is dimmed. Sunlight piercing the clouds expresses both the warmth and the otherness of God; light that is unimpeded, and indeed known only in what it strikes, expresses God's immediacy and

See
Plate
1

---

[2] Newbigin, *A Word in Season*, p. 198.

[3] Ruisdael's Christian background is explicated in John Walford's *Ruisdael*. Light is, of course, an important symbol for God in the New Testament: 'I am the light of the world' (John 8:12), and 'God is light, and in him is no darkness at all' (1 John 1:5).

immanence. The fascination of these images is that they are not symbolic code, but inherent in the creation, and to that extent out of the control of the artist. They do not even need to be consciously expressed, but are part of a shared perception, in which one is unaware at which point the artist's vision ceases, and the viewer's begins. The Creation, seen unself – consciously in community, and attended to under the broad 'permission' of knowing that it comes from God, in both its created and its cursed aspects, allows of discovery. Doctrine rightly used, liberates vision rather than limiting it.

One such moment of discovery in landscape art came, ironically, when all doctrine seemed to have been blown away, as 'Christian civilization' slid into self-destruction in the Great War. Not 'creation', but unimag – inable destruction faced the 'official war artists', as they struggled to give meaning to what they saw. This was not a place, of torn trees, pounded mud and rat-occupied corpses, where any shallow belief in order could survive. But the stubborn witness of the great paintings that came out of the unthinkable horror, is to beauty. Even among the suffering masts of trees, and shell-holes luridly reflecting sunsets gashed in the sky, there is nobility, there is suffering that is noticed and has meaning. We are unmistakably in the theatre of God's world; even when the bruised artist has renounced any facile belief in God.[4]

See Plate 2

Moving from landscape to portraiture, in the study of the human face the question of a real good Creation is posed even more sharply and more intimately. The overall concept of a fallen Creation pales before the subtleties of the individual case, where the artist must find his way in the tidal overlap of good and evil. Two of the supreme masters of portraiture seem particularly at home in this precarious middle ground.

As a child I used often to look at Rembrandt's self-portrait in London's Kenwood House, a picture which gave peculiar comfort in the way it seamlessly joins greatness and frailty. It echoes everyone's vocation to

See Plate 3

---

[4] Paul Nash, an artist reared in the British Romantic landscape tradition, wrote a famous and moving letter from the Front, describing the sense of God's absence that he found there: 'We have all had a vague notion of the terrors of battle . . . but no pen or drawing can convey this country . . . Evil and the incarnate fiend alone can be master in this war, and no glimmer of God's hand is seen anywhere. Sunset and sunrise are blasphemous, they are mockers to man, only the black rain out of the bruised and swollen clouds all through the bitter black of night is fit atmosphere in such a land . . . It is unspeakable, godless, hopeless . . .' But of course 'godless' only has meaning by reference to the 'godfulness' which should be there, just as the power of Nash's pictures arises from the dialogue between devastation and beauty. See Richard Cork, *The Bitter Truth*, p. 198, quoting from Nash's *Outline, a Fragment of an Autobiography*.

**See
Plate
4**
glory, with everyone's painful self-knowledge. Later on the portrait that
came to fascinate me was Velasquez's *Pope Innocent X*. Ironically, this
picture is probably more familiar today in the distorted rendering of
Francis Bacon, in his Screaming Pope paintings. Bacon's paintings are, of
course thematic paintings, not portraits, but it is hard not to think that
Bacon is missing, or refusing, a general truth that Velasquez has seen.
Bacon's 'scream' places desperate emptiness at the heart of authority, a
pitiful hollow mouth where there should be a human being who claims
to know something, especially something of God. Velasquez does not
appear to suffer from these expectations; but neither does he repudiate
the dignity he finds. At the root of Bacon's vision, I take it, is an anger
and disappointment at the absence of what he partly believes should be
there, the ability to know God, disproved, symbolically, by Velasquez's
unsaintly pope. But his anger has created pictures which are, in effect,
statements of a position, rather than free observations.

Velasquez, however, has entered that 'middle ground' where he does
not seem to be looking at the face of the Pope according to his
expectations, but lets the man glare out at us, with his strength and
weakness. Velasquez's steady eye is not that of the disappointed idealist,
but of one who is not fixated with power, and is prepared to look behind
the mask with both realism and love. His penetration of authority, by
being ready to see both greatness and obtuseness interwoven, has a
continuing power to shock which we may find lacking in Bacon's more
systematic view.

Creation, then, seen under the impact of the Fall, is not a concept to
bludgeon the world with, demanding of it perfections which it may or
may not be willing to provide; nor is it a romantic idealism which is bound
to disappoint. It is more like an idea with which to capture fleeting
impressions of goodness. *That flash of blue over a stream; have I really seen a
kingfisher?* If I know what is likely to be there, I am more likely to believe
it when I see it.

The history that has gone

Seventeenth-century artists, of course, lived in a very different world to
us. The existence of 'the Fall' as a historical event had not been seriously
questioned. Today the most prevalent concept of 'the Fall' is the failure
to evolve sufficiently to surmount the teething troubles of humanity's first
few hundred millennia. The idea that there was a state of being which
was better, in all except technology, than the world we have now is one
which seems to make little sense historically, even if the idea of an original
innocence is still lodged in the collective memory. Yet without such an
idea, it is very difficult to think of any real duality in creation, such as we
have said that artists have perceived, dividing what is there from what
ought to be there. What we have is what we have, good and bad, and it

is pointless to moralize about it. It is all one thing, and 'good' and 'bad' cannot possibly apply to what nature has simply thrown up, in her efforts to propagate and survive.

I cannot see how one can avoid wanting to know 'what happened', because that is simply another way of describing 'what is', which is the fuel of art. In any case, it is 'AD' which has given us 'BC' and our curiosity about all the steps backwards in time. But in asking historical questions about Creation and Fall, we do need to be aware of how we are weighting different kinds of evidence. Velasquez and Rembrandt may have intuited something which our modern intellectual constructions would miss. These are difficult questions, especially for the scientific layman, but in facing them it seems to me that at least four kinds of evidence should be balanced.

a) The incompleteness of cosmology
The impression is sometimes given by scientific writers that time can now be observed in an unbroken visible track, from our own times, back through Darwinian evolution, to the Big Bang, with no stations or derailments on the way, neither Garden of Eden, nor Fall and Curse. But this description, mostly in the form of chemistry and rather large numbers, of how we got here, should not be confused with explanation, that is to say, with saying what we are and why we are here. No kind of numerical explanation can in any way anatomize the pope of Velasquez, and say what makes him so humanly human. For that we must look to issues like creation, corruption, and calling. But these issues do not somehow hang in the air, separate from genetics and other aspects of the pope's human anatomy and biological history, which ceased at death. If those 'theologi - cal' characteristics are there, they are there as part of his human history as well. If being 'created' and 'fallen' is part of his character, it is part of his (distant) history as well. The Big Bang theory, while so appealingly making a front door to history, must not be allowed to be a juggernaut, destroying every other concept, as if it provided any sort of explanation for the issues that culture has unearthed over centuries. A grand unifying theory of physics is still only physics; there is a physics of this book, and every part of culture, which in no way explains what it means or why it is here.

b) The limits of archaeology
I wonder what the world would be like if there was an archaeological museum in which genuine traces of Eden, pieces of the original unspoilt Creation, were displayed. It might seem to suggest that there was a stairway back to perfection, and that our right to set eyes on such things had not been forfeited. Whereas the fact that there is, as far as one knows, absolutely no trace in the ground of a Creation that is different from what we have now, though disappointing from the point of view of hard fact,

contains the symbolic truth, that that whole world of innocence is indeed closed off. Whatever happened to the world to make it the mixed place that it is, happened completely, and the 'angel with the flaming sword' preventing return to the Garden (Genesis 3:24), sealed it absolutely, even to archaeology.

Which leaves us with the world now, the world of art, for our understanding of creation. Or does it? What of our desire to know history? Do we have only the contrast between the 'hard fact' areas of cosmology and archaeology, which do not answer our questions, and the 'soft fact' areas of art, or indeed of faith, which gives us a subjective understanding of the world as it is now, but with very little to pin it to? Hard or soft (which, after all, are also matters of taste), we need to remember that there is only one question, which is 'what sort of world do we in fact live in?', and we can only have the kinds of evidence appropriate to the world that is there. What we need is not so much the rigid application of hard fact criteria, as a guide to what is around us.

c) The priority of miracle
A guide is more than a theory, it is a way of looking which reveals what is there. If we consider simply the New Testament (and then use that as a light, if we wish, on Genesis), it would seem that there is far more to the world than contemporary physics has yet taken account of. [5] Miracles, for example, used to be thought of as 'breaking laws', as if laws were in ultimate control, and exceptions were almost super-real. But clearly Christ did not come as a law-breaker, but as a teacher of other laws – laws of faith in God, which his disciples learnt slowly, and which are still imperfectly understood. These laws must have significance for our understanding of Creation.

The Nature miracles, in which water was changed into wine, loaves multiplied, and water made stiff enough to walk on (?), as well as the healings, imply the possibility of an equally 'creative' original Creation. Though Jesus in a limited sense worked with what was there, he also demonstrated the power to originate, making new matter (e.g. more bread), by faith in the resource of God's mind and will. The resurrection re-creation of Christ's body further shows the provisionality of 'natural' processes, reversing entropy and demonstrating the complete subjection of matter to the Spirit of God (Romans 8:11). These are windows into

---

[5] It is always interesting to see what dogmas are handed on to children. 'Since everything in the Universe is made of matter, we can say that matter is subject to various physical principles', *Children's Britannica* asserts (1988, vol. 11, p. 243). Unless tautologous (all matter behaves like matter), this sounds like an assertion that there is nothing but matter. *Britannica* says nothing about the possibility of matter itself being further subject, to *spiritual* principles, which is the issue in question here.

processes we cannot pretend to understand. But we must allow a due sense of shock to take hold. This might shake us free of the assumption that what physicists understand is all there is, and allow us to see far more immediacy in the creative will of God, than the picture of the remote organizer of the Big Bang explosion would allow us to conceive. When Jesus called forth Lazarus from the tomb, he wanted him alive: by so 'tampering with' (in fact subjugating) natural processes he showed that life for people is his effective, personal desire in general (to be fully effected in the 'general' resurrection at the end of time). God is as immediately involved, as creatively and personally involved in the continuation of existence, as that.

What we have in existence, then, is not the unmarked debris of an explosion, however it 'happened', but a wanted world, in which matter matters.

d) *The distraction of Darwinism*

If we are wanting to learn to see the Creation as meant, as wanted in all its aspects by a personal being, it is worth mentioning that we may have to unhitch our thinking from the restrictive hold of Darwinism. There may be various ways of doing this, from reconciliation to outright rejection,[6] but we need consciously to address the fact that to view life-forms solely under the concept of a reproductive mechanism, chance edited by circumstance, is to 'grey out' much of the world's colour and pleasure. Belief in God, as deliberate, immediate Creator, allows us to appreciate the beauty of the world as intended – trees were made 'pleasing to the eye' (Genesis 2:9) – with nature designed not just functionally, but for well-being (Genesis 2:18) and enjoyment (Acts 14:17). The concept of 'survival' as the main motor of life, though perhaps an echo of the reduction of existence after the Fall to a more basic level (Genesis 3:17–19), would seem a rather depressed response to the joyful command to 'be fruitful and multiply'. The choice we have is to join many philosophers, thinkers and, it must be said, some of the least attractive political leaders, in taking our meanings from what is at best (that is, if true) only a natural process, so falling into the worship of nature; or to allow the higher, God, to define, and if necessary to expand, the understanding of the lower, through which we can see life in all its created freedom and splendour.

---

[6] Books and articles abound which try to reconcile the God of the Bible with the processes proposed by Darwinism. Frankly I think there is some strain here. The story-line of Darwinism, which is perfectly well understood by its proponents, is at face value very different from the story-line of the Bible. However, there are signs that the hegemony of Darwinism is itself under threat, from within science. See the ground-breaking *Evolution: a Theory in Crisis*, by Michael Denton.

The Bible that has been displaced

Our discussion of the historicity of the Creation will have brought to the surface the issue of the Bible's status. Without arguing the issue, it may be productive to remind ourselves that we also have a choice here. We can restrict our understanding of the world to that which science can ascertain; but then our art also must be confined to the certainties – and uncertainties – of a scientifically-mediated nature. Meaninglessness will be a 'fact' of reality. Absurdly, a sense of meaninglessness is in practice not a condition that favours existence, certainly not human existence, which perhaps makes it rather a doubtful 'fact'. Alternatively, we can recognize that there is much that we need to know that science cannot tell us, which is nonetheless 'fact', but communicated by God in the way that persons do communicate, by *word* and *act*. We need to understand, in other words, that the Bible, which is almost too normal for us, is also normal for God. This may help us to a more open and personal reading of the Creation.

* * *

To summarize, then, our main difficulty in seeing the Creation in all the different dimensions which the character of the biblical Creator implies is that we stumble on Creation's mixed messages, and in so doing are tempted to retreat into the 'safety' of abstract, and artistically less fertile, concepts derived from science. These concepts begin to take on a spurious priority over their own subject matter, from which the Bible alone can deliver us, if we will free it from the same subjugation to the culturally dominant, but partial description of reality provided by science.

Chapter Two

Culture: Biblical Backdrop for Art

Having tackled some of the mental 'debris' in thinking of Bible and Creation, we can now try to survey art from the eminence of Scripture. We are not forgetting that, in many ways, this seems an odd thing to do. After all, the arts are there, in every city and every home, but as for the Bible, if we know anything at all about it, it is that the arts do not greatly feature. Painting, as a form of image-making, is of course absent, music is represented in worship, but we do not hear of Jesus taking his disciples to a concert, or of Paul relaxing at a play. So is it not stretching things to be looking for guidance in a book which has principally left the arts, and very successfully at that, to fend for themselves?

Just how 'successfully' the arts are functioning at the present time, is of course the matter in question. We cannot come to the Bible usefully unless we have felt the dependence of the arts on a broader structure of meaning, for which technological hope of our age will not suffice, and been aware that the life of the arts, for all the energy in the 'arts industry', has to come from beyond the arts.

But it may still seem strange to try to start from first principles and ask 'why culture'? Most people do not have to give themselves permission to listen to a record, or visit an art gallery. Such radical questions belong only to such times as conversion, when one's whole structure of assumptions may be dismantled and checked over, or to periods of national, and economic, self-questioning. 'Why culture?' then becomes a question in which simple reference to pleasure and recreation suddenly seems inade - quate to the issue. Why must Mozart be played again and again? Why must children do ballet lessons? Why should money be spent on architecture? Such questions of justification seldom seem to generate appropriate answers.

The more solemn one becomes in justifying culture, the more its value seems to evaporate, and an unexpected ambivalence surfaces. It is not just the modern era, or the puritan conscience, or the question of public funding, but something about culture itself which seems to make it at once necessary and superfluous, both life-giving and stagnant. So perhaps we do need to question the place of the arts in the scheme of things, and come to the Bible with a duly humbled sense that it may, after all, show us something that we need to know.

In this second chapter, we are particularly trying to look at Creation as that something that *implicitly* generates culture (or the arts). We will approach this by thought experiment, of doing some 'digging' and imaginary construction in Eden, and then, following the New Testament, by trying to get a peek at Creation as it was formed in the studio. Out of each of four sections arise some clear principles for art.

Culture always intended

The arts arrive in the Bible without fanfare, slipping into its story almost unobserved. Jubal, a descendant of Cain, 'was the father of all those who play the lyre and pipe', and Tubalcain, his half brother, 'was the forger of all instruments of bronze and iron', some of which, given Lamech his father's violent and vengeful nature, were probably weapons of war (Genesis 4:21–24). It was out of another line altogether, not Cain's, but Seth's, that came the ancestry of Christ (Luke 3:38). If the arts have an early beginning, it is not a particularly auspicious one.

The slight ambivalence in Scripture about the origin of the arts, occurring without comment, but without commendation either, may partly explain why our conception of Eden is usually rather more raw than cultured. Indeed, as we said in the first chapter, we find it difficult to update 'Adam' into any kind of man we know. Not for him the restless masculine energy to carve up the planet; the conquering passion to reshape everything, to turn everywhere he sets his eyes on into a human home, moulded by his mind, and in his image. And yet all these things, ugly though they may be, and misdirected, do stem from creation. They can be deduced from God's much misunderstood, and sometimes misap - plied, command to humans to 'have dominion' (to which we will return). Instead, our normal, essentially static, picture of Eden tempts us to relate everything that has to do with activity to sin; especially the sort of free, creative decision-making involved in art. Goodness relates to unsullied nature, sin to the artificial and the intervention.

Whereas, if we learn to think of the disturbed and enjoyable world that we have now as what God created, it is that much easier to relate the arts to him and to his intentions. And assuredly God did make humankind to do things. Humans, of all creatures, are only complete and themselves, when interacting with their environment. A small boy is seen to be 'more himself' when astride his bike, attempting stunts. People are known by what they do. You do not really 'see' a human, as a person on their own, without their works. Even portraits, which with all subtlety focus the marks of life left on a face, often express the works as completing the person, providing all manner of props to suggest their active life. Humans are, essentially, extending creatures. The fur or plumage in which they are so lacking, and which expresses so much in their fellow-inhabitants of the planet, finds its equivalent 'extension' not just in clothes, but in all the complex of relationships, their work in ideas, their influence and authority, and the physical work by which they make their mark on the world. The beauty of the human animal is only in a small way limited to its appearance.

God made people to do the things that people do. We will need to look at misdirected activity, in relation to art. But it is not, as we tend to think, that Eden (seen as permanent holiday) was the normality, and work (intervention in the world) the aberration. God let people loose to think up culture in all its forms.

Disneyland – God's Creation?

'Culture', of course, is a funny word, especially in England. No one is quite clear whether it is a word for elite leisure pursuits, or whether it is a broader word for everyone's social habits. If we say it stands for everything that makes us human beyond the bare necessities of life, that includes the arts (it also includes football); but it allows us to see that the arts may have wider connections than a merely aesthetic concept might lead us to expect.

Perhaps to represent all of culture, we might be permitted to take for a thought experiment, the example of Disneyland, which no one would accuse of being exclusive high culture, but which evidently fulfils an innate, and apparently compulsive cultural function. If we try to imagine Disneyland in Eden (for all I know, 'Eden' may be viewed in Disneyland), I think it becomes clear that culture does have an essential, if surprising, place in the making of the human home. So, take your seats for a unique cultural-theological spectacle.

Culture mediating nature

The first reason that we have taken the step of inviting Disney into Eden, is not that Eden needs beautifying, (and if it did, we would probably go to another decorator's), but that Eden's existence as pure nature *cannot be received fresh from the packaging, without concept or comment* . It is not 'home' without some connection to the human story, and we need to relate what we find in Eden, plants and animals, to our story. Garish plastic may not be the answer, but fairy tales brought to life in imaginary castles, sea-voyages, or jungles, help us to see many dimensions of existence, and all the different parts we can play in it. Through culture, we also learn the language of Creation, and see 'lofty mountains', 'rushing rivers' and 'trembling leaves', where without it we might just see inert matter. Through story, we step into possible modes of engagement with the world, trying on different characters, and appropriating their responses to nature. Plants and animals that have become part of a story, as every children's writer knows, are seen in quite a different relationship to humans, and hardly less productively, than those seen only through the eye of science.

Culture questioning nature

That is not to say there is nothing odd about Disneyland. But if there is, there is also something odd about human culture generally. We have pictured culture (of a sort) in Eden, as being sympathetic to nature, helping through story to bond us to it, to make us at home *in our minds*, as well as physically. But culture generally has no automatic sympathy with nature. Indeed, relationship with nature is what it is there to question.

If we picture the contrast between animal 'culture' and human, the difference is apparent. Birds build, dance and sing, animals sport and play: there is something going on in nature that seems undeniably beyond necessity. But it is part of these creatures' being, their way of life. With humans, our culture has much more to do with our questioning of life. Do we belong to nature?

Should we try to be 'natural', or artificial? A Chinese classical garden brings nature, in stylized form, right to the brink of the home. A French seventeenth-century garden places untamed nature at a distance, but it is mediated through graded levels of cultivation. Compared to the artificial court existences of ancient China or monarchic France, our modern social lives are all 'untamed nature'. But, whether one thinks that we have become 'natural' because nature is no longer a threat, or whether it is that nature has overcome, and enticed us, behaviourally and ethically, into imitation, nature is still a point of reference for the fashioning of the human identity. Being human is to have the choice whether to go with it or against it.

Culture, then, represented by Disneyland, is something that we can see as part of creation, though it can appear as a problem or a question. But being a question is not intrinsic to it. That aspect of culture, which anxiously, or defiantly, tries to 'place' us in the physical realm, by defining the human image in relation to nature, derives from our condition as alienated beings, searching for our true identity. Are we a frail Chinese pagoda, perched above the abyss, open to the winds? Or are we a Palladian mansion, placed squarely in nature, commanding all it sees? Or are we a Corbusian villa, landing like a spacecraft, self-contained and alien?

The 'meaning' of Disneyland

What Disneyland represents is another matter. A real castle has some inherent symbolism. The taking of stones is an exercise of dominion over nature; making them into walls of protection is part of warring nature's language. It is not surprising that a castle has 'image power', as a more than utilitarian building, with a capacity to signify that has made it a strong cultural theme. But a plastic castle? That has more to do with the refraction of meaning for distinct cultural ends, and especially those of commercial culture, in stripping away all sense of dread from a castle, leaving only saccharine romance. The way that a castle articulates nature, and the expression of power over it and over other humans, is left at several removes. Indeed the idea of Disneyland relating to nature as it actually is, rather than to fiction-based concepts of nature, is almost an absurdity. The whole idea is to produce a total man-made reproduc - tion world, in which fantasy is realized. Such a human home, not in nature, but apart from nature, has an enormous drawing power, as if we have got to see what sort of world we ourselves can create. It does not matter that it is second-hand, commercially-processed nature: it is ours. How can dull old nature's subtleties compare with the certainties of modern plastic?

Culture as human being-in-nature

What can this mean in terms of the original Creation and God? It means first that we are very unusual creatures, with a creative drive to make worlds within worlds. Not just happy to settle under a hedge or tree, we must make exclusive spaces by which to define ourselves. We feel we need boundaries between ourselves and nature. Such assertion of distinc - tions, going back to Genesis, may be some of the implications of God's having made creatures 'in his own image'.

This is true of any architecture. It is true of a garden Wendy House, that it is a world within a world. But did this principle have to result in Disneyland? The fact that we might want to cover his world with acres of plastic shows some of the risk God took! But there is no actual need to shut nature out. If, in some sense, Disneyland is antagonistic to nature in its exclusive artificiality, then it (and many other places with less imagination and humour), is not implied by the original creation. There can be a human home without antagonism. Disneyland, in seeming to turn its back on nature, shows that nature is still asking us questions we do not wish to hear. It is not that we have to be nature. Nature itself, with its need for tending, allows us to be different. But nature, in who it comes from, and whose character it shows in the way it is made, points us beyond ourselves to someone greater than us. This may be why it is that, for all the asserted love of nature, our culture's behaviour towards it is often aggressively antagonistic.

All relationship involves a measure of interference: being who we are, we cannot be in nature without, in effect, using some of it to define our identity (artistically or otherwise). But things go wrong when that identity has become a question. Nature then becomes an issue and, by self-preoccupation or by downright antagonism, Creation suffers abuse.

Genesis now – creativity and its limits

Having tried to bring Creation up to date, and having seen that it does really refer to the world we live in, and not just to a primitive world in which no art was possible or desirable, there is still the question of what we can learn from the Bible's account of creation, of what art should be trying to do.

Creative temperament and the Bible

Here we find that art is at the centre of a dilemma as to how we should 'be' in relation to God. Some godly people instinctively suspect any human exercise of creativity to be an act of defiance, an infringement of God's prerogative. For them, the mode of being that is appropriate to us as creatures is close obedience, not having our own ideas. For others, the idea that God might have ideas about what we should do, is an infringe - ment of our creativity. We were born free. Being given blueprints and instructions is anathema. So, how should we 'be' in relation to God?

We could caricature the two conceptions by likening them to the factory and the art school. In the factory, the worker must use the tools, and follow the designs exactly as instructed. Any exercise of personal creativity will halt the production line. It is bound to be seen as rebellion. Some authors have given the impression that God's commands are like that. The problem is, that for the creative person, there is nothing very appealing about merely executing someone else's designs. We call such work mechanical, less than human. In the art school, by contrast, the goal is undirected creativity. Instructions for specific projects belong to the learning stage. Energy is supposed to come from inside out, rather than as a response to requests from top down. Between the two extremes lies the performance of music, which needs fully-involved humans to execute it, with all their freedom, and commitment. But this helpful analogy does not entirely dispose of the anxieties of the artist who wants to be an originator, and who may not wish to play only the scores that others have written. (Some would say that playing God's 'scores' enables you to be truly original yourself. It will certainly have you doing what you have never done before.)

These sorts of questions are critical for whether artists and the Bible are going to get along. If art is, in itself, rebellion, an attempt to refashion a created order already sufficient and perfect, this book need hardly be continued further. If however art, as a human contribution to the scene, is what was envisaged by God, then we have the much more complicated task of seeing how that freedom can be genuine, and still within creaturely limits. Those who are 'artists' by temperament may still resent the idea of there being limits. Therefore we shall have to explain how those limits are really none other than the limits, or rather boundaries, of our being as humans.

This may sound cold comfort, but it is fundamental. A spider always remains a spider, a crab a crab, and an ape an ape. A human is the only species which seems to think there is no upper limit on what it can become. Many of the physical and mental boundaries have been broken down. But we will always be humans, whose upper boundary is being 'not-God'. That makes limits, not only to do with such minor matters as omniscience, and omnipresence, which technology tries to overcome, but most tellingly to do with our 'position', that our rule is dependent rather than ultimate. A limit is different from a ceiling, because within it is the comfort of being what you actually are. Within the outlines of our design, we can live to the fullest (the very enjoyable fullest) capacity, *and not experience being not-God as a problem*.

Therefore we can be comfortable, as artists, in not having the burden of re-thinking existence; and accept, rather than disdain, an attunement to the existence we have.

Art as subduing

When we bring these sorts of issues, of freedom and restriction, to the Bible, what do we find? Starting with the first chapter of Genesis, we find, before we encounter any restrictions, humans placed in a world which needs 'subduing' (verse 28 commands them to 'fill the earth and subdue it'). That is something we can relate to. As in so many adventure stories, personal identity is to be discovered as we tackle a task. We become human as we get going. The world is not a static display, with no room for us except as admirers. It is more like a child's box of bricks, or Picasso's junkyard, waiting to be assembled. 'Subdue' implies mind over matter, the human will organizing, and, it is implied, pacifying, something unruly, which is not yet what it should be.

But does 'subdue' imply making it whatever we like? This may be where modern ideas of creativity and the Bible begin to diverge (and we are only at verse 28!).

Subduing, though it contains a strong hint of repressive force, implies *removing the discord from a situation*, so that it may function peacefully according to its own nature. It is the idea of getting something to work, rather than taking its components and making it into something else. There is no hint, in God's commands, that the world needs recreating by humans. It needs setting in order, not a fundamental rethink. One reason for this, surely, is that though the world could have been created completely fine-tuned, and needing no further attention, God desired to bring his creatures, human and otherwise, into relationship with it. In particular, he designed people to become fully themselves by taking decisions in the world. They could not be creatures 'in God's image' if they had nothing to do.

However, if we agree that the human task was, by definition, one of completing God's own purpose for the world, according to the nature he had given it, that implies that nature offers us an overall framework. As we work with it, its own nature tells us what to do. Our subduing work is one of discovering what works. All this seems to suggest science rather than art. But at this stage, they are surprisingly close. There is a parallel with picture restoration. A picture restorer is both scientist and artist. Leaving aside the chemistry involved, in analysing the materials of a picture, the restorer as objective scientist has to work out what in the picture is missing. Its own appearance discloses a lack. But then as artist, that lack has to be recreated imaginatively. Something new has to be made which fits. (I was once in a public gallery, and overheard a distinguished art historian explaining that most of a quite well-known painting, which he had discovered, was by the restorer. I believe he said the face prominent in the painting was the restorer's self-portrait! To me it had looked an admirable seventeenth-century picture.)

Our interventions in nature have the possibility of congruity. *We can do things that fit.* The business of art is indeed not with restoration as such. But art does have the possibility of such a sympathy with nature that what it does enhances it. This is most obviously true of architecture. There are many landscape views that only become noticeable because a church or house articulates them. But even painting, insofar as it creates environ-ments of the mind, can either turn its back on, or else go with the grain of, the creator's overall plan as disclosed in nature. The question of nature and its meaning is always there. Any interventions we make in nature demonstrate how we respond to it. A beautiful bridge, for example, is more than engineering. It is uplifting to look at because it recognizes that the world we live in is more than functional. Its careful proportions, daring trajectory and soaring crossing lead us, not only into part of the world, but into the idea of it. Its instinctive good design is also good theology.

Art as naming

Subduing nature, though it sounds too horribly like the fate of the rain-forests, is inherently cultural, because it always involves having a philosophy in relation to nature – at the least, whether to be 'natural' or 'artificial'. But there is another activity, given to Adam, which seems even closer to art.

Then the LORD God said, 'It is not good that the man should be alone; I will make him a helper fit for him.' So out of the ground the LORD

God formed every beast of the field and every bird of the air, and brought them to the man to see what he would call them; and whatever the man called every living creature, that was its name. The man gave names to all cattle, and to the birds of the air, and to every beast of the field; but for the man there was not found a helper fit for him. (Genesis 2:18–20, RSV)

Sometimes this task of naming the animals is presented as if it was Adam's scientific, daytime occupation, a coolly objective exercise. But as de - scribed in the story, it is part of Adam's search for a wife. God observes that the man is lonely. Then he creates the whole gamut of the species, with the implication that they are there for relationship with the man. Then he brings them all to Adam to name, not as a job, but so that Adam can find out what they are (and how well they relate to him). The name he gives them is not just an arbitrary linguistic label, but says something about what they are. This is why God says 'whatever the man called them, that would be its name'. The name was to signify the thing itself, as understood by the man, as he made relationship with it. The task of naming is also part of Adam's search for *self*-understanding. As he looks at each kind of animal for companionship, he discovers that he is something other. Only another human being (but not his mirror image, or he will still be alone) will do. God sees his plight, and the next creature he names will be Eve.

The process of naming, as Genesis frames it, is extremely helpful in freeing us from a view of knowledge, and of art, that lurches between the poles of objective (and obedient) or subjective (and creative). There is something almost disturbingly creative in Adam's activity. Whatever name he chooses, God will stick with. The name is the man's choice. He commands it, and thereby makes some boundaries round the creature's identity. But although his personal understanding and creative powers are involved, in thinking up appropriate names, (as in the punning name for 'woman'), it would be futile if his naming was arbitrary. It would also have been very exhausting! Anyone naming would soon run out of arbitrary labels. The story seems more to suggest that he studied the creatures, so that the names could say about them something that he had observed. There is no division here between creativity and objectivity, because one is a necessary response to the other. [7]

See
Plate
5

---

[7] Art has long been under the shadow of an objectivist view of knowledge, in which the idea of the person is left out. This view of knowledge was challenged by the philosopher-scientist Michael Polanyi, in his *Personal Knowledge*. For an excellent account of its importance for art see, *Voicing Creation's Praise, Towards a Theology of the Arts*, by Jeremy Begbie, e.g. pp. 234–243.

The idea that pictures were chiefly intended to contain information had already been rebutted by John Constable, who in a memorable phrase said 'the art pleases

Art as knowing

We see, in Genesis, humans placed in a world in which persons need to find things out. Information-gathering, knowledge, encyclopaedias and libraries are to some extent a creative activity. Why and how we organize information is for us to decide. It is part serious, partly a game. It is serious in as far as we are managing the world; it is a game in as far as God is ultimately in charge. The fact that he is in charge allows us to make choices not compelled by necessity as to what we will study. It gives us great pleasure to exercise this freedom, to study the stars and put men on the moon.

But curiously, there was given to Adam a command about something that he should not study. That something, a tree, appeared to hold the key to knowledge, not just as information, but as the wisdom which holds the key to all understanding.

> The LORD God took the man and put him in the garden of Eden to till it and keep it. And the LORD God commanded the man, saying, 'You may freely eat of every tree of the garden; but of the tree of the knowledge of good and evil you shall not eat, for in the day that you eat of it you shall die.' (Genesis 2:15–17, RSV)

There is something intriguing about this tree, the fact that we do not know exactly what is meant by it, and this fascination is partly the point of the story. Adam and Eve wanted to know too. Many temptations offer the bait of more information or experience. Experiences and knowledge cannot be un-had. In the story, God knows this, and verbally guards the man from the fruit of the tree. He warns the man of the dangers, rather as parents today warn their young about drugs. If they do not try, they must trust. The antidote for temptation is trust.

We can put the story round in a more positive way. The fact that Adam and Eve had to exercise trust in this instance, shows that they had been created as information-hungry creatures. The measure of the temptation is that they were in a world in which they did not know everything. Their knowledge-lives had to be made. This is significant for Christianity and art.

One of the offences of a certain presentation of Christian intellectual culture to art is that it behaves as if life has no further questions. But art is partly a process of finding out. How do story, and beauty, and ugliness – truth in the physical and spiritual worlds – connect? If everything is

---

[7] *(continued)* by reminding, not by deceiving'. The purpose of a painting, in other words, is to point away from itself to a reality beyond it, rather than trying to 'contain' the reality within it. The artist's perception (personal, subjective) is the means to 'remind' of the external world (objective). See Plate 5.

settled, that aspect of art becomes redundant. That is not to deny all that is settled in Christian truth. For every article of doctrine, and the rest of mind it gives, one is unceasingly grateful. But in living into that truth, there is plenty to find out. There is no lack of questions, no end to the quest to 'place' ourselves. The Bible, for all its certain affirmation, admits to some obscurity in truth. Einstein's famous comment on physics, from his Jewish understanding, was 'God does not wear his heart on his sleeve'. In the New Testament St Paul said of Christ, that in him 'lie hidden all the treasures of wisdom and knowledge' (Colossians 2:3, REB). There are treasures *hidden*. And, as St Paul said elsewhere, 'now we know in part' (1 Corinthians 13:12). At the centre of it all is not a tree but a person, whom we can trust with the things which we do not know.

If it is true that as creatures, we have been made to be always finding out, but never knowing completely, that gives a good reason for art. Art is a way of knowing, satisfying but incomplete, from where we are, and this is the boundary, not just of art, but of all knowledge. No one, neither scientist nor guru, is going to crack the final code, and make further attempts to understand a waste of time. No one will bust us out of the prison of partial, creaturely knowledge, to gain the light of universal truth glimpsed outside. For then we would indeed be 'as God' – and have responsibility for it all.

Whether this was the form Adam and Eve's temptation took is another matter. The lust for divine, universal knowledge, the opposite of trust, could well have been what lay behind the desire for fruit to 'make one wise' (Genesis 3:6). But what they got was knowledge of the other side of life, the unlooked-for possibility of *undoing* good, knowledge from which God, like any parent, wished to protect them. 'The man has become like one of us, knowing good and evil' (Genesis 3:2, REB). Unfortunately, unlike God, he was not always so good at distinguishing the two. From that time, there comes into knowledge an issue of discernment. Good and bad must be discriminated in their different disguises, and we, the viewers, can be as deceived as those we study.

There never was a universal fulcrum of knowledge, for Adam, for Aristotle, or for anyone. But now, added to creaturely limitation, there is sinful partiality. Knowledge has become something of a thieves' kitchen, with no arbitration and everyone (all the religions and philosophies) laying claim. For art, this means not that we abandon the search for truth, but that we recognize how far ourselves we are implicated in untruth. We enter the art gallery, metaphorically, on our knees.

The Creator's developed style

We move now from what we learnt of art from Adam's situation, to what we learn from the visible Creation itself; but still guided by the biblical account in what we look for. Apart from Genesis, there are glimpses of the meaning and processes of creation throughout the Bible, especially in the book of Job, in the Psalms and in Proverbs in the Old Testament, and, even brighter glimpses in the New Testament, in John's gospel and also in Paul's letters.

St John's account, like a doorway into the revelation of Christ, is written in formal imitation of Genesis, opening with the absolute state - ment, behind which nothing but revelation can take us: 'in the begin - ning'. But the difference from Genesis, and its expansion, is that John takes us into the inner workings of God, into the relationships of the Trinity. In terms of the creation, we are allowed to go from the public showroom back into the artists' studio.

As a prologue to his gospel, John's initial purpose is to tell us who Jesus Christ is; what he was before he appeared as man. This is almost too big to read about. It is like suddenly taking the sunglasses off and looking at the sun. We are almost glad the passage does not last very long! and that we can soon enter into the human narrative of Jesus. Jesus, 'the Word', *is God*, who has always been there, 'with God'. And as God, the Creation is also his work. For the purposes of John's gospel, this is to tell us what to begin to look for in the life of Jesus. For our purposes here, it also tells us to look for something in Creation.

> In the beginning was the Word, and the Word was with God, and the Word was God. He was in the beginning with God; all things were made through him, and without him was not anything made that was made. (John 1:1–3, RSV)

What then, in these verses and the following ones, are the qualities to look for in Creation, now we can think it together with the name of Jesus?

The name of the artist

'*All things were made through him*'. This statement is reminiscent of one of the Renaissance or Baroque studios: Rubens in Antwerp, or Bernini in Rome, who might be asked to make anything from a whole building, to a theatre set, to a silver salt-cellar. In every production, small or large, we look for evidence of the artist's mind and touch. Nothing leaves the studio without his approval. He has designed and made it; he is committed to it. His name goes with it. However small, it is 'a Rubens', 'a Bernini'. We might feel embarrassed to say of a piece of Creation 'here I have a Jesus', but that idea at least enables us to see it in a new way. We can see it as fully intended, as something with personal mind behind it, his mind, the one who wills goodness. We would see it as having not just a character, but a quality.

There is, however, always a limit to how much the works tell us about the artist, because an artist works as someone doing a job, fulfilling a specification: Jesus shows himself the skilful workman who is able to realize, say, the insect's needs, rather than 'express himself'. But, that understood, thinking of Jesus enables us to see aspects of the quality of the work, which lie within the boundaries of his divine character as we understand it.

Next, John repeats himself: *'and without him was not anything made that was made'*. His emphatic statement leads up to the fact that the Creation does not receive its own creator. But there is *nothing* that did not come from him in the first place. Any work of art is subject to its maker; the artist has rights over it, at least until it is handed over, and the dealers and restorers get at it! But the authority of defining the work as full and complete belongs with the author, and the author has the right to correct it. In respect of the world that we know, John's gospel asserts that there is no power in it that was not originated through, and under the full authority of, 'the author', Jesus Christ. This has weighty implications for what the Creation is like, should be like, and the lengths the author will go to, to put it right. And it is understandable that he wants to get it out of the hands of the 'dealers' and 'restorers', and back into his own hands.

The quality of his work: and the critics

The next phrases sharpen up the issue of a quality in Creation, because it is a quality that can be chosen:

> In him was life, and the life was the light of men. The light shines in the darkness, and the darkness has not overcome it. (verses 4–5)

In these few words, John is beginning to give us a picture of Creation which is radically split. On the one hand, there is in it a certain particular quality, which comes from God, which he calls both 'life', and 'light'; two metaphors, conveying all the energy and purpose that makes us live, and all the understanding and intelligence (moral intelligence) we see by. He has given Creation to live, but not to live and blunder about, but also thoughtfully to see. But, on the other hand, there is also an opposition. There is darkness, in which there is neither life nor understanding. The darkness appears to have an energy of its own, which tries to overcome, but cannot, or tries to 'comprehend' (Authorized Version of the Bible), but cannot. As we would punningly say, there is something 'dense' about the darkness.

This is the true opposition for which we should be looking in art. There is a light and life that comes from the hand of the master. The spiritual connoisseur learns to recognize it. In this we are not just talking about the Creation, but also about what the Creation produces. 'The life was the light of men.' There can be something of the Creator's style in their work. He has designed them, not only to have functioning bodies, but to have 'light' in their understanding. Intelligent, truthful, inspired work is, then, quite 'natural'. But something profoundly unnatural has happened; darkness has become the habitat of women and men. No longer is the light all around them; they have to look for light.

This truth is severe, but it is also freeing in relation to the opposition with which the world of art is occupied. We ask of anything, as the categories get wider and wider, *'is it art?'* If it is, we give it some sort of privileged response; indeed usually, a very privileged response, including fascinated media attention. But the true opposition to which we should attend is: *'is it light?'* The beginning of St John's gospel is already aligning us to make choices. The Creator's style is very particular. His work involves light, life, and necessarily truth and goodness. Everything origi - nally belonged to that style. Eventually, all will be restored to it. Which shall we choose?

There is another way of putting this question which, at this stage in the book, may be of more immediate use to those of us looking at art. We *may* choose, we are free to choose; we are asked to have an alignment in terms of ultimate values, and this takes priority over the insistent presence of art-world values.

Created not just for us

From our brief look at the Creation in St John's gospel, we have arrived at what may be quite a dramatic reorientation. We have learned to see the created order in a new way, as intended, wholly purposed by a good God. Matter, once (we thought) begotten as 'an accident', has all the loved look of wanted offspring. Therefore we may be drawn towards nature, and wish to emulate its qualities in our art; those qualities that we relate to our knowledge of Jesus. That conception of Creation from his hands turns us towards nature. But we may still see nature as consumers see it, and get its whole purpose and character out of proportion. We need a further jog to our understanding.

St Paul, having made his own meditation on the relationship of Christ to Creation, adds a small but significant point to what we have learnt from St John. Writing to the church at Colossae, to whom he had much to say about the exalted status of Christ, and its implications, he writes: 'all things were created through him *and for him*'. The 'all things' are revealed to be, not just the physical world:

> For in him (Christ) all things were created, in heaven and on earth, visible and invisible, whether thrones or dominions or principalities or authorities – all things were created through him and for him. (Colossians 1:16, RSV)

The geology, the flora and fauna whose 'origins' so worry us, occupy a fairly small part of the whole, whose centre is Jesus. Their purpose and focus is bound up with him. This means that the truth of the Creation, the fact that it has discernible qualities which delight and excite us, points not to us and our needs, which we can disregard at will, but to one who cannot be disregarded.

The truth of Creation has transcendent authority for us, because it points to God's way of doing things. And it is doubly authoritative for us, because we too have been created 'for him'. Our orientation is therefore not so much towards nature (in loving respect and emulation), as through nature towards Christ. That should make us able to see nature, neither in self-centred romantic ways, nor in sentimental 'natural' ways, which inevitably are projections of our own ideologies, but in a crisply focused otherness, which we are really able to enjoy, since we know the one around whom the whole universe revolves.

Over the centuries, there has been a lot of perplexity experienced among followers of art as to whether to make nature normative. Is the reproduction, or imitation, of nature what art should really be aiming at? It has seemed difficult to express the dominion of humans in Creation (represented, loosely, by the Classical stream) if we have to make ourselves subject to what is going on in nature (the Romantic stream). But when, as here, we look into the behind-the-scenes events of Creation, we discover that this dilemma is false. Both human life (with one set of responsibilities), and natural life (with a different set) are intended to look towards Christ. The attraction of nature is that, to a large extent, it still does. But we cannot re-direct ourselves simply by becoming 'natural', not unless we accept the focus of nature. The point for us is to discover the philosophy or mind behind nature, and to be influenced by that.

★ ★ ★

The consonance between art and nature that would create harmony instead of discord, in lifestyle and culture, comes about not by copying nature, but by a restoration of the human mind to the kind of life and understanding that it was intended to have. The unity between us and nature is focused on Christ. This is why, in the end, we can confidently look for a *creative complementarity* between the works of humankind and the works of God. The best architecture is, in a sense, not at all like nature; but it fits with it as the appropriately human complement.

We have seen that the Bible's teaching necessarily implies a choice of light over dark, a re-oriented mind in art as in everything else. We can see something of it in Christian history. When we try to imagine it, however, it can still sound somewhat restricted, severe or religious. But there is a picture of it given in the Old Testament book of Proverbs, which shows it in its true creative and playful nature. It describes Wisdom,

who in the New Testament is exemplified by Christ, working together
with God on the Creation:

> When he assigned to the sea its limit, so that the waters might not
> transgress his command,
> when he marked out the foundations of the earth,
> then I was beside him, like a master workman; and I was daily his
> delight,
> rejoicing before him always, rejoicing in his inhabited world,
> and delighting in the sons of men. (Proverbs 8:29–31, RSV)

The world of evil and nothingness has its attractions for the artist; but
when we get up into the world where Christ is at work, there is such
a health and sufficiency to it that that other, false and negative world is
forgotten. That is the call of the Creation. It is a call, rather than
something to copy. But it is not so indistinct that it does not have clear
meaning for us now. To try to distinguish some of those specifics will
occupy us for the next chapter.

Chapter Three

Natural Art

In this chapter we will look at something which gets as easily taken for granted as Creation itself, and which also fits easily alongside it; it is the free art, the normal art, most frequently recognized in the crafts; art which is so basic I am calling it 'natural art'. It is natural, as we shall see, both in that it is like nature, and also that it is natural to us; if we are free to go along with our natures.

But what of fine art? Is there such a big difference between natural art and fine art as perhaps we had assumed? The real goal of this chapter is to show that, as far as Creation is concerned, there is no difference between natural art and fine art, except a difference of levels.

For this conclusion, history will not of course support us. The ideology of art, from the time of the Renaissance, the decline of the guilds and the rise of individual artists too big for them, has progressively seemed to detach the dignities of the fine artist from the craftsman. The modern conception has grown up of craftsman and artist, of one as obedient to a task, and the other as free. The artist initiates, while the craftsman performs. But if this is really the case, then history has let us down, and detached the artist so much from his roots that real art, as something that is both craft and creativity, has withered. Theology, rather than history, supports a different view, which is that in Creation, there is only one kind of art: this is the natural art of fitting form and given meaning, which has its own inherent, created structures. Of course artists want to play with these structures and push them around; but it is out of the dialogue (to put it politely; but it ranges from fascinated conversation to outright fighting) with the created structures that the manifold communications of art, ancient and modern, take place.

Identifying natural art

What is the natural art we are referring to?

I am thinking of pots, and things like that — and flower arrangements, and cakes: ordinary things that make life good. Natural art, like many of the good things of life, should be easy to find but is oddly elusive. Unlike well-made, mass-produced electrical goods, which it is almost impossible not to buy, it has to be sought out. Finding it, indeed, is part of its delight. It is the exotic art of Indian crafts imported to the West, in boxes, bowls, cushions, jewellery; each piece suggestive of an interesting story of origin, a picture of markets, of shadowed huts and sunlight, of family, costume and traditions (*but not the factory*). It is the art of pottery brought home unscathed from a Portuguese market; souvenir gourd-vessels or baskets from Africa or South America. It is the universal art of the museums, the kinship of the craftsman across many centuries and cultures: English decorated slipware from medieval times, Islamic bronze pots, Roman wall paintings, coins, and altars. It is also that which it is the objective of many a craft club to produce, and many a harassed Christmas shopper to find. But as has been lamented at least since the day of Ruskin, the conditions of industrial life, and impersonal market economics, are as corrosive to natural art as the smogs are to the Parthenon stones, or petrochemical plants are to Venice.

Why 'natural'?

I am calling this art 'natural' because it arises in all societies, and because it has an obvious resonance with nature. It is not that it copies nature; it is very distinctly human. But when you see it, it shares with nature those two qualities which in natural things we take for granted, but which in art are rather hard to produce. First, it has an *obviousness*. 'Of course' this pot should look like that, just as of course this oak or elm leaf, or that extraordinary tropical fish, should look like that. It is not that they are not, when you think about it, utterly surprising; it is that very soon we are convinced, almost to a point of loyalty, that that is how the thing should look. Its shape, and decoration if it has any, belong to it.

A second quality goes with that obviousness. Like things in nature, this art looks as if it should be free. *Free as a plucked berry, free as a toe-dip in the sea.* You would expect to have to pay for something weird, or artistically unusual, but this art that is merely 'right', which is as it should be, has the look of being there for the picking. This must be particularly annoying to craftsmen, who are often forced to sell what appears to come freely to them for ridiculously low prices. But it is paradoxically true, given the rarity and difficulty of such art, that things which are so much as they should be, so perfectly, obviously shaped, so joyously decorated, like nature, seem to belong to no one and everyone. This insight may, it is true, rationalize a habitual lack of generosity towards the craftsman; but there may also be in it a pre-theological perception that art of this kind is a gift, and that there should be an abundance of it for all.

Is it natural for humans to be 'natural'?

Natural art is very normal, *but of course you may not want to be that normal.* If we want natural art, we find that, from the (self-conscious) human point of view, it follows certain conditions. In other words, it has a defined form, with boundaries: to which one might respond with acceptance, enjoying the space inside, or resistance, convinced that they are a limitation.

Picture yourself put in charge of a garden. It is a very beautiful one, of the 'stately home' variety. It has pathways, steps, yew-hedged enclo - sures, arbours and ponds, and at key points are huge stone vases on plinths, carved with figures in the Roman manner.

You are imaginative: the dark yew hedges excite you, and you quickly visualize trailing flowers against them, with just the right colour and size of petal; in another part, you plan a subdued, shady area of greys and grey-green foliage as a contrast to the bright main borders. And so on. What you are doing is 'natural art'. The two characteristics of what you are doing are discipline and freedom.

There is no doubt you are under a discipline. You cannot do just what you please. This is not because the owners say so, but because the garden says so. It is the garden that tells you, in your imagination, what you need to do with it. By taking on this garden, you have placed yourself under aesthetic obligations. There is no avoidance of the aesthetic frame. Imagine also a blank space in the garden, where a tree has just fallen down. It is the space that makes demands on you. It was not in your contract to fill it. It is the gap that cries out for remedy. But it is through freedom that you fill the gap. Imagination tells you to put something there that has never been seen before. It is a new idea, perhaps startlingly new in terms of this garden. But it is 'right'. It fits perfectly, and helps you see new qualities in what is on either side. Obligation does not tell you how to be free; but it is freedom that keeps the work of art alive.

So much for gardening. What about the Roman-style stone vases? They too are 'natural art'. In one sense, there is nothing natural about them. No one needs giant flowerpots with handles which would never be used, and dancing ladies sculpted round the side. But the garden needs them. As massive objects they help you see and relate to the big spaces, to know that the garden is in stages, and that the small border you are looking at relates to a larger whole. Their silhouettes, at once controlled and flamboyant, help you see both the sculptedness and the naturalness of the trees. Their fine carving gives you a moment of focus on the human world, to which all this tamed nature is subject, before you immerse yourself afresh in greenery and flowers.

The vases have been brought to the garden, following the 'laws' of obligation and freedom, because they were the artistic solution to a need. But their creation, maybe in some mason's yard hundreds of miles away, also followed the same principles of natural art. Your look at their extravagant curves, first bulbously convex, then elegantly concave. Of course, you register, they have to be like that. One answers the other. But how was this balance of forces intuited? Was it a sudden inspiration, or did it take decades of trial and error to work out? The inventor of it was under the authority of an aesthetic obligation. It had to come out right, almost with the rectitude of a machine that must work; but it took all his imagination to do it, imagination and freedom to dare to be so striking, to give so richly.

'It can't be anything else, but how was it arrived at at all?' These, then, are the features of natural art, art which is the human counterpart to the works of nature, something both normal and utterly mysterious. But there is one more feature which natural art shares with nature, which is so implicit that we only see it by contrast with art of other kinds.

Natural art and hierarchy

Take a look at our stone vases again, standing proudly beside the stone steps, leading you up like a guard of honour. They are utterly splendid, worth much more than a moment's glance, but they are also *subject*, they have a particular place and weight in the scheme of the garden, and no other. They do not try to control you. They have their place, and they allow you to pass on and do whatever business you have with the garden as a whole. They are a phrase in a symphony, wonderful to listen to in itself, but with a job to do which gives them an office they cannot exceed. They are subject, not just to the idea of the garden, but to the whole rational-aesthetic order out of which the garden derives its beauty.

This idea of place, a place in the hierarchy or scheme of things, is something we are not a little sensitive about in these democratic and self-assertive times. We like everything to be equally important, whereas the idea of hierarchy allows that, though the smallest part may be equal in value, there are parts which command and articulate the whole in terms of key and scale, whether the organization is a human one or an aesthetic one. This crucial feature of natural art is that it has the power to be subject to a larger whole. Our imaginary vase is a powerful work of art in its own right, which would grace any museum, but it does not destroy it to give it a function in a larger scheme. Rather, giving it a job to do will bring it to life.

But are you not just talking about decorative art? How can you expect us to take seriously an argument based on a pair of garden ornaments? Of course decoration has to fit in with its surroundings, but what has this to do with art? There is a common prejudice against decorative art, which may be related to this issue of hierarchy, and our sensitivity to it. Hierarchy does not destroy value, but that is something which we need to relearn.

a) On not apologizing for decoration

The assumption is made today that if art serves a function, then it is no longer fine art, art for its own sake. This idea is rapidly transferred to the artist. The artist whose talents serve, is no longer the true artist. The true work of art has no job and no context. It makes its own context, and the job of curators and others is to serve it. The work that did have a context, that did serve, is an embarrassment in the art museum. This division between contextual art and free art is so real to us that it appears to make it possible to despise stone vases or indeed garden statuary. But it is historically, and aesthetically, nonsense. Michelangelo's greatest work was done for a decorative context. The slave sculptures, for example, were made for a projected tomb. The Sistine ceiling itself is a vast scheme of decoration, which the artist did not despise to design. It is also a superb exercise in hierarchy, in which, it is true, the artistic scheme began progressively to burst its bounds. Art as something self-existent is an invention of the museums (but with an important spiritual pay-off, as we shall see in the next chapter). In its natural form it is anything but self-existent; instead it is the imaginative way of responding to external realities, which may include physical contexts as well as truths and ideas. Michelangelo is just the most prominent example of an artist who saw no difference between art and decoration; and this, we can deduce, is for an important aesthetic reason.

When we think of hierarchy, it is so often with an idea of the lower being completely subjected to the higher, as if it had no freedom or independence within its own limits. Perhaps we apply the idea of totalitarian despotism to art, thinking there is no middle ground between being totally controlled and completely free. But within aesthetic hierar - chies, it is absolutely essential that each level functions *as art*, that is, with both obligation and emancipation. This is why so often the 'conservation style' of architecture fails to do any good, in, say, a street in an aesthetically or historically sensitive area where a gap needs filling. The timid conser - vation style building tries to be a nothing, a meaningless blank, instead of an independent work of the imagination, and ends up as an eyesore. A building, like a person, needs to be something positively rather than to try to deny its own existence, which in the end (perhaps also with people), causes more trouble. We can see the value of the 'positive presence' in our example of the stone vase. Its power to dignify and articulate the garden is not simply as a hunk of masonry of a certain size, but as a work of art, in which the vigorous and subtle way in which the stone has been 'brought to life' carries its own message about human and natural being. It is as a living part of the whole body of the garden that it functions.

It could be that it is this same misplaced sensitivity to hierarchy that has led to the arts of decoration being relatively starved of talent. Two outstanding decorators nearer our own time were the American architect Louis Sullivan (1856–1924), and the Spaniard Anton Gaudì (1852–1926),

whose uninhibited ability to take their gigantic schemes right the way
down to tender detail is so refreshing, when compared with the near-focus
barrenness of so much architectural design today. [8] But decoration, however despised in one generation, seems to be felt as a vacuum in the next;
and we have begun to see a revival in our own time.

b) Hierarchy and meaning

It is easy to identify an artistic element, such as a vase, as taking its place
in a visual and spatial scheme. But we have said that our vases take their
place in a whole 'rational-aesthetic order'. In other words, there is a
proper subjection of the art object also to an agreed realm of ideas.
Hierarchy, the place of the part in the whole, also has an 'invisible' side
to it, as art fits into a given reality of concepts. How does this work?

Natural art is as breathable as the air (should be) in the landscape; we
can entrust ourselves to it as art, because it has settled into an external
order of *meaning* that is simply there. This kind of art object is as reliable
as technology, and indeed goes further. Technology can be reliable in
accurately articulating potentialities of the physical world: a tall building
can stand on daringly thin *pilotis*. But technology may reflect an extremely
tenuous grasp on what it is wise to do with those potentialities, in the
world of meaning: the same building may be ugly nonetheless. However
the natural work of art takes its reliability also from the realm of ideas;
those perceptions of reality that are part of the common experience. The
true work of architecture (thinking of it as natural art, not as 'stunt'
architecture) can take responsibility for itself not only in the technical
sphere, or the aesthetic sphere, but also in the realm of common
understanding. It has no inhibitions about employing a universal language
of intelligibility; as with a building that looks as if it shelters, an entrance
you can find, walls that enclose, etc. These all go beyond practicalities to
the unselfconscious needs of signification.

Turning again from architecture to the kinds of artefacts we see in
natural art, such as sculptures found in burials from places as far apart as
Egypt and China, we have no difficulty in entering a meanings-world
that is recognizably common, not contrived. A Chinese clay-modelled
household, or a carved Egyptian fisherman, invite a sympathy that comes
from a shared sense of life under the seasons. But if, mentally searching
the museums for other such objects, we ask how much common
experience our widely different religious and cultural outlooks actually
produce, that may be a partial explanation for the comparative scarcity of
natural art. Natural art is not trying to invade or shape the given order.
It is not magic objects, or the talisman of a philosophical quest. It has the
capacity to rest in the scheme of things as it is presented; nature, domestic

---

[8] A very eye-opening account of how decoration works is to be found in John
Unrau's book, *Looking at Architecture with Ruskin*.

life, government, war, universal conditions. That may make it sound neutral. But given the human capacity to contest the idea of a given scheme of things, natural art, far from being neutral, is extremely potent. However before looking at the meaning that natural art derives from its sometimes controversial participation in the given order, we must look further at its content.

The content of natural art

We have seen that far from being a very 'subjective' activity, in natural art *the artist becomes subject*, sometimes quite reluctantly so, to the disciplines of the work. The freedom comes about in trying to work out how to fulfil what the work demands. This has further implications for the content of the work.

The paradox of the artist, the originator, also being servant to the work has an instructive counterpart in the human giving of life. Just like a parent, the artist may at times be exhausted, emptied out; but see in the health and individuality of that which has been produced a proper transfer of energy, a fruit of labour. And just as the typical characteristics of the well-loved child could be described as healthy (or tended) form, character, and provision of adornment, so also the natural work of art's content could be described as *form, character* and *adornment*.

We can see how these different elements work together, if we think again of the craft objects we started with, for example a pot, a dish or a jug. In principle, at least, the artist first reaches out to give *form*, the overall shape that enables an object to be one thing rather than another. She does not try to make a universal kitchen utensil, amorphously part-plate, part-jug, part bowl, but a choice has had to be made. In being one thing, certain other possibilities are closed. That is its particularity, a choice that has, as it were, been made for it. There is an obvious parallel with the particularity of the Creation. If it wants to have a universal significance, it has to start by being local.

But having form, which allows it to do its job, it is also given *character*, to do its job in a particular way. Now whether it is a squat jug, or an elegant jug, may not greatly affect its function, but having such a character enables it to take a full place in the human meanings-world. It might be a jolly little jug for homely teas, or a tall refined one for formality. Character comes about through the maker seeing the object freely, as something that wants to become something, in a rounded kind of way. Identifying with the object's need to 'be something' is, perhaps, not unlike acting, where you allow yourself to 'be' someone else. In this case, the unique personality of an object is liberated through the artist.

Then somehow, to take the third element, this whole process needs to be crowned with *adornment*. I say 'needs to be', though obviously you can have the finest of steel or silver jugs that is perfectly plain. But their absence of decoration takes its meaning, its elegant concentration on line and surface, from a context in which the normal response to the creation of something fine is to adorn it. The sensation involved in decorating an object, whether it is framing a picture, dressing a child for a party, or even doing what the advertisers of diamond jewellery would like us all to be doing at Christmas, is that of giving it (or her) honour, an appearance of being cared-for and publicly valued. However 'primitive' such behaviour may feel, it seems to be a principle built into Creation. Jesus himself observed that 'God . . . clothed the grass of the field', that is, decorated it with flowers, and he drew the conclusion 'How much more will he clothe you, O you of little faith' (Matthew 6:30), with more than a hint, looking at the fields, that God's way of clothing was not of the cheapest and meanest.

The dignity of the maker
But natural art also has a hidden content on the human side of the equation. We have stressed the paradoxical sense in which the originator of the work of art is, in the process of making, also subject to it, and has to 'get it right'. But the subjection of the creator to the object is not slavery. (There may be economic slavery, but that is a separate issue.) The well-known phrase from the Book of Common Prayer comes to mind, about the Lordship of Christ, 'whose service is perfect freedom'. On the contrary, the fact that the creator of an object, who gives it form, and character, and honours it with adornment, has developed a relationship with it, actually confers on him or her a particular dignity. The craftsman, the maker may be poorly paid, but he is a person of standing. His standing somehow comes from his humility in bringing new 'creatures' to life. He or she is recognized as a person of self-discipline and service, who has been prepared to enter into the objective world where things must be made to work – even artistic things. The true professional, for all the freedom he or she has to invent entirely new solutions, has the dignity that comes from accepting a responsibility for outcomes in the public world.

Natural art, like nature itself, has an objective quality of working and playing its part in the public domain. We do not say that the public world is entirely its judge, because the leaders of opinion can be corrupted out of their own responsibilities, but that there is a world of public responsi - bility and public truth is something that natural art recognizes. It is this truth that seems to be represented in that fertile Old Testament proverb: 'Do you see a man skilful in his work? He will stand before kings; he will not stand before obscure men' (Proverbs 22:29, RSV).

It may seem strange to emphasize this point when today almost the reverse seems to be the case. What 'skills' today stand before 'kings'? Certainly some presentational skills. But there is a vast gulf between the performing skills honoured in the world of classical music, and the unclothed egos who have captured centre-stage in the world of art. The principle is nonetheless a correct one, (which shows how far from natural art we have got), that what the craftsman loses in personal display, he gains in dignity; that natural art, though it may lack notoriety, has a natural honourableness.

The meaning of natural art

There are a number of social institutions, marriage and family being among the most prominent, which seem to mean something beyond themselves. They are things which, humanly speaking, we could never dream up, and which have their own internal laws to which we have to fit ourselves to make them work. And the way they work, when they do work, is mysterious and beyond comprehension. What, for example, is the intangible unity in difference that marriage, at its best, expresses? It seems to point to some higher order outside it. Natural art is likewise one of those things that are easier to grasp than to understand, and which are satisfying partly because they point to an order or meaning beyond themselves.

So let us, once again, take hold of, say, an African basket which someone has kindly brought back for us from holiday, and try to consider why it is so satisfying. It has character, and shape, and it is decorated – what does all this mean?

Uniqueness is allowed

First of all, taking our basket's characterful shape, it speaks of a world in which characters are allowed to exist. This is not a totalitarian world, in which every variation from uniformity is stamped on. It is a world in which difference is recognized and accepted. In her moving account of China under communism, *Wild Swans*, the author Jung Chang describes how women, in styling their hair, would exercise their minds to inventing the very slight variations from communist convention that they could get away with, where any show of character was liable to be dubbed individualistic or bourgeois. On the broader scale she recounts the tragic destruction, under the same anti-creative impulse, of the nation's artistic past. Wherever natural art shows itself, it subversively speaks of a world in which the particular has its place, and not just a mechanical place, but a breathing, personal contribution as something of its own to offer.

It is a fact that a lot of this kind of art nonetheless comes from societies with very little personal freedom. It may be that our own cherished autonomous freedom is not as healthy for art as we think. However, rather than looking at African, or oriental-style despotisms, for example, as beneficial for art, we should probably look at this art as showing a permitted outlet in such societies for freedom. More importantly, the point about the institution of art, as of marriage, is not what it shows about the society in which it is embedded (because the society, in some measure has to conform to the institution), but what it seems to show about the goodness of the transcendent world (i.e. heaven and God's pattern for this world) to which that society should be conforming.

Security, freedom and belonging

Turning back to our African basket, there is also a meaning it conveys at the human level. The maker who can attend to the shape and decoration of such a delightful basket is a 'settled' person, whose own needs for personal recognition have been met. Established in the world, his atten - tion can be fully focused outside himself. This also has a transcendent quality, because in this world no one is that secure, either materially or emotionally. It is more a security that is intuited, as the craft object or work of art is attended to. The maker is a person of value who belongs, and he conveys these properties to his work. Oddly, he probably finds his sense of belonging as he works, and feels part of some bigger purpose than the task in hand. I do not know whether such an experience would generalize, but when I try to paint, having overcome fear or inertia, it is as if some bigger impulse than my willing has taken over, and I am not so much doing a job, as finding myself part of a job.

There seems to be a further, extraordinary, transcendent truth, that the craftsman stumbles upon, and that his or her work conveys — *our freedom is part of a bigger will*. The things we do freely, at great cost, which we have never dreamed of before, turn out to be, when we have done them, things that had to be done. Part of this is that the rightness of our pot, or picture, is something so outside ourselves that it is as if we never thought of it, but it was there all along. This may account for the fact that not doing art is far more painful than doing it. There is a sense of so many things that are there not having been done. Bringing things to birth is rather less under one's personal control than our normal concept of autonomous 'creation', but it is probably a lot nearer the reality of creative activity.

Another part of this sense of our art being part of a bigger will has a parallel with nature. In nature, the birds and beasts, rocks and trees, have the quality of being utterly themselves, and yet utterly willed. They are created and free. In our terms this is a paradoxical quality. We find it very difficult to hold together theoretically the idea of the real freedom of creation and that God is willing his will through it. But this is something that we experience in art, as our freedom builds into God's order, and something we see in nature, as in freedom the whole has a power of cooperation with God: the lively sunsets that speak volumes to the attentive eye, or the call of a blackbird in the evening, that rescues us from cares.

The quality of blessing

These 'transcendent' qualities of natural art, the sense of valued particu -
larity, of security, and of freedom combined with an almost uncanny sense
of having been appointed, could all be summarized in the one word *'good'*.
When God made everything, he saw it was 'very good', as Genesis tells
us. That is not how everything appears to us, however. But the qualities
of natural art speak of a world of meaning in which things are not mere
things, but have been seen, made and valued as 'good'. Just as the 'pure
natural goodness', which the supermarket manager would like us to
imagine in his factory-produced bread, conjures up images of a homely
Victorian mother baking at the kitchen range, so the things of Creation,
and works of art that share those natural qualities of discipline and
freedom, speak of a given goodness, that is associated with the good will
of the Maker. The Bible word for the active, personal endowment of
goodness and goodwill on a being or thing is 'blessing'. Natural art has,
in short, wherever it is found, and in whatever age, *a quality of blessing*.

What we are daring to say here is that the work of natural art conveys
more than the fact that its human maker has blessed it, though it should
at least do that. It is that in some way, like the works of nature, it also
seems to be caught up in the transcendent purposes of God. How do we
pin this down? Is it that God wills his will into us as we work? Is there
some endowment of Wisdom for the maker? At the very least, natural art
has about it an irreducible quality of something happening, as much as
something we do, so much so that the artist is compelled to stand back
and exclaim: 'I made that, and where did it come from?'

'Natural art' and fine art

Natural art at a different level

If you make a cake, ice it, and put cherries round the edge, that is craft,
and you are clearly working within the limits of natural art. The shape
of the cake tells you roughly where to put the cherries. If you wanted,
you could go in for some extravagant patterns, but given the decorative
tradition of cakes you would probably be limited by the demands of
symmetry. But suppose you made a cake through which you wanted
to say something a little more universal than 'nice cake', and you varied
the expected language of cakes in a very deliberate way to give a certain
noticeable inflection, you might just be moving into the realm of fine
art. You are still relying on the framework of language provided by
natural art, but the meaning (and it had a meaning before, associated
perhaps with love, care, celebration) has become more complex and
deliberate.

Much of what we normally recognize as fine art is still on a continuum with a cake. A gilded medieval altarpiece is not so far removed, in conception of craft finish and freedom within limits, from a masterpiece of a cake; and, moving still further up the scale of complexity, the erstwhile pastry-cook Claude Lorraine has not dissimilar business to do in bringing his tirelessly resolved landscapes to completion. The distinc - tive 'art' quality is not to do, then, with oddness in respect of form, or any revulsion from the demands of craft, but more to do with using form and craft to higher levels of expression.

A common language

That the differences between craft and art are marginal is best seen against the immense witness of nature, the chief language-provider for both art and craft. It is nature which teaches us to see and express through form, which educates our eyes and teaches us to make demands on art. But does nature today still exist, in any integrity, for this background language to work? Characteristically we see nature today in sections, parcels of green, squares of sky, selections squared-off for the TV screen. The British artist Patrick Caulfield has brilliantly captured, through his hard-edged interior scenes, what it is like to live in an almost artificial world. But even city life with its packaged nature has its escape routes.

You can travel thousands of miles through the doors of the local tropical fish shop, for example, and come face to face with the underwater life of sea anemones, clams, plants which might be animals, and curious and exotic fish. It is like an imaginary look at God's own workroom where, like a master toymaker, he has delighted to construct humorous faces and movements, and to colour them like rugs, porcelains, marbles and jewels, as if they had been made purely for his own pleasure. There is hardly a single fish, one finds, in classical 'good' proportion; but in the variety played on that implicit theme, everything is proportioned well, proportioned to express its own peculiar character. You could fault one, or you could fault them all, or you can enjoy that sense of having been almost deliberately teased which shows that you are truly alive in God's world.

If, then, you multiply this one experience, admittedly a selective one, across the whole of nature, it is a fact that an aesthetically ordered, yet utterly varied and delightful world bears in on us very strongly, and is the whole background for art. Even where you would least expect it, nature presses in. Today, travelling in an aesthetically hapless Midlands city, I see a tall block of flats, poorly built, almost colourless, a repetitious pile of square windows with pinkish surrounds against bare concrete. It looks marvellous. Low cloud, or fog, depending on your frame of mind, makes it almost melt into the grey winter sky, while a pale light, reflected in the windows, faintly glows, in gradual counterpoint of glass against wall, as

the building rises. This building should not look good, but it does. Nature
is witness both against it, in its loveless monotony, and for it, as a
wonderful reflective surface for light. Nature sets the terms, and very often
adjudicates, or mitigates, the result of all artistic effort. But because its
principles have been internalized by us, who are, after all, part of nature,
we do not consciously think that comparing art with nature is what we
are doing.

You could call the aesthetic language of nature a kind of 'law'. This
is not an imposed set of rules, but simply those energies that situations
seen visually disclose. It is no one's fault, for example, that a rectangular
frame sets up certain dynamics, so that a mark placed within it will appear
to be stable, falling, rising, leaning, depending on where it is put. This
language simply derives from our being upright creatures in a gravity-
defined world. Sometimes we react as if there was something conspira -
torial or authoritarian about these given languages, but it is healthier to
regard their givenness as the external code that makes communication
possible. We do not have to prove that all such signs mean exactly the
same for all times and places, to see that they do have a remarkable
communicability. Art is, after all, rather easier to teach as a universal
language than English or Esperanto.

One could devote much time and space trying to lay out the aesthetic
and emotional language of nature, as did Ruskin, and more recently the
Gestalt psychologists, with the danger that the exceptions that always
appear in such a complex system, compounded by individual judgement
and taste, tend to over-impress, and lead one to wonder whether a
building or painting can communicate anything at all. But the fact remains
that, perfect language or not, this is the system we have, and there is no
alternative to working with both those things that are secure and those
that are more relative. This system, which works as well as art works,
undeniably derives from the total visual education, in form that appears
charged with meaning, that nature (yes nature, poor bruised nature)
provides.

The meaning of nature: received and refused

For our purposes we may say that the language of art, that we read through
from nature, and through craft, to art, works mainly according to two
principles. There is the visual framework and vocabulary we have already
mentioned, which includes reading form anthropomorphically, such as
looking at a tall, droopy tree and thinking it looks 'sad'. We have, then,
an emotional language of form.

Then there is a second grid arising from the implicit ('transcendent')
language of meaning. We have spoken of the way the craft object, like
the works of nature, may seem to carry a meaning of belonging to a 'good'
creation. If we take this quality as something like a spiritual appeal that

inheres in nature, then obviously it will arouse reactions, positive and negative. Some will like it; some will dislike it. There is no compulsion to like good nature, any more than there is a compulsion to like good people.

We could take two influential examples of *diverse attitudes to nature*, though they are not usually compared. The writer and illustrator Beatrix Potter, in her ability to humanize animals and yet to be true to them, is someone who was more than content to work within the tradition of belief in Creation; it is the idea of a benign personal mind implicitly behind nature that makes such jumps of imagination, the hedgehog as washerwoman, credible. Her very style invests animals, and landscape, with that loved particularity that we have mentioned so often. It could be that it is her illustrations, absorbed by many of us at a young age, which has so enabled us to identify that quality in nature for ourselves.

Whereas, when we turn to the work of one of the most creative modern animal artists, Picasso, there is a sense of theological equivoca-tion, to say the least. His real fondness for them comes through in his drawings and sculptures, but his animals and birds have a much more elemental, impersonal quality, as if no centred Creator mind behind them was being sensed or acknowledged. It is almost as if they are being re-conceived as denizens of an independent, energetic but empty and unfathered world. We will need to discuss further the spiritual resistance that can be provoked by nature and art. Here the point to be agreed is that craft and art both enjoy the same frameworks of meaning and expression, but that in art these become more highly charged, or indeed contested.

Form: accepted, contested

a) Titian as a natural artist

However it will not have escaped the notice of any readers familiar with modern art, that there is something old-fashioned, indeed 'old hat' about this discussion. When we look at a Raphael or a Rubens, it makes perfect sense to be talking of natural art as the normal and healthy impulse to perfect form; but it is also obvious that we have some generations of artists for whom that activity is redundant. We must repeat here that the issue is not that of the 'fineness' of fine art. The issue is more to do with a fundamental acceptance of language.

See Plate 6 In a late Titian, for example, like the furiously brushed *Death of Actaeon* in the London National Gallery, we are not talking about any precious desire on the artist's part to produce expensively crafted commodities. Here is a dramatist in paint, at the peak of his powers, where thought and gesture break through uninhibitedly, without self-conscious concern for finish, into a realized vision of tragedy; and yet the instruments on which these chords and discords are played are the traditional ones – of three-dimensional space, the pull of forces in a rectangle, the metaphorical power of nature, light and atmosphere – in short, Titian's *own development of the language of natural art*. Careless of polish and detail, he still cares, as he did in those early years when proving himself on the intensely-laboured *Bacchus and Ariadne* (also in the National Gallery), about the relationships of part to whole. He has to, on his own terms, because he is an artist.

b) Breakdown of the codes

For Titian, the language of natural art was simply a means to an end, rather as this sentence is to me as writer. I have a duty to organize it in its classical form, of subject, verb and object, otherwise it will either make little sense, or you, the reader, will be distracted by what seems a blatant omission. Within the classical form, on which the partnership between writer and reader rests, there is of course considerable latitude to play and otherwise make exceptions, provided that the central agreement does not break down. You want my language to be transparent, so that it does not get in the way, and you can think through it to my meaning. The final comma, and the artist's final touch, releases the work to be a vehicle for meaning, which all being well will speak back to the author or artist as well.

However with much modern work, that agreement, which is found in classical form, has broken down, so that the language becomes as much the subject of the work as what it may be trying to say. When looking at, say, some of the abstract sculpture of Anthony Caro, William Tucker or Philip King, there are undoubted emotional resonances to be hazarded, and some conceivable rationales to what has been presented, but the registering of visual relationships of part to part does not seem a very important consideration. Colours and shapes start to have references outside relationship, which it is necessary to enter a particular thought-world to decode. Facing some of these challenging puzzles, one is left with the sense that to look for a visual harmony represents a rather disreputable appetite, as if it was right to rebuff the senses. But rigorously artificial as their world is, these sculptures cannot exactly deny the language of nature. For what other sort of language is there? Things are seen in relation, even if they are not exactly made to be seen, but thought about. The relationship with nature of this art, then, rests either on some complex kind of inversion (of our most natural impulses), or on a deliberate repudiation of nature, or in an attempted replacement of it. The theme of nature is still the unavoidable background, although you could say it is avoided by being ignored. My concern is not, of course, that these works are abstract, but that they seem to push beyond the boundaries of the normal language of making. This does not prevent their being art, but it might make the viewer long for more of that of which they are the negative image.

c) Denigration of natural art

It will be argued, however, that there are many forms of art today, conceptual art or the art of installations, for example, for which my model of 'natural art' is simply not relevant. There is, after all, no attempt in them to make an art object, and any form they have must be experienced on the level of ideas. There may be much in this, but it does not explain how natural art, the aesthetically experienced whole, is alternately deni - grated, and experienced as a thorn in the side, by the exponents of this kind of art. For them, natural art seems to represent *something that has to be countered*.

I am myself not at all in favour of a sterile conservatism, in which the 'harmonious whole' becomes an end in itself. As we have seen, the true natural art is something that intrinsically serves, and points beyond itself. But I do agree with what I think these modernists discern, that natural art does indeed represent a certain meaning. They may think of it as representing a conservative ideology. It is strongly likely to have 'conser - vative' connections, because of its relationship with continuity and tradition. But if it is an ideology, it is one of which you might find elements in conservatism and radicalism as well. Natural art hints at the fact that we are presented in reality with something which stands over against all 'isms', a given order, in which part and collective are valued, and none are absolutized; for all are accountable to the one Creator.

Fine art, form and meaning

It is not, then, intrinsic to the idea of fine art, as opposed to craft, to be awkward about form, traditional language or natural metaphor. Fine art may well be fully immersed in the given languages of natural art, but use them, as we have said, at a higher level of meaning. *What we really have to look at is not the popular distinction between craft and fine art, but between two different ideas about art*, one of which attempts to turn its back on nature.

To many, who have seen the historical undermining of nature seen as Creation, this latter seems the only responsible course. They must attempt to construct an entirely human world. But to others, who find this work so much less satisfying as art, a question arises. If natural art is so successful, maybe (despite its antiquity) it is not based on a false premise, or indeed hints at a false promise. Perhaps the art that people the world over are drawn to, in all periods, from infant learner to mature craftsman, which is so like nature, also has something to say in support of nature. Art as creation reflects back on nature as Creation.

★ ★ ★

It is a solemn mechanical world that Darwin has left us, and a world of intellectual trouble that many of the conceptualist artists infer. Sometimes, if I may say this, I want to leave them to their troubles. 'If God so clothed the grass of the field . . .', said Jesus, who had used his eyes and drawn some shattering conclusions. Some of these were to do with the irrele - vance of anxiety. There is a lot more to this world than some of our artists immersed in troubles allow themselves to dream of. The joy we are permitted here, despite the mess of which we are a part, the joy from sun glistening on corn, or the blue of the sea, is a joy that will be echoed a thousand-fold when we see the solution to all ills that is planned in heaven. Art has to it a touch of the power of God to bring life where there was none, to redeem, to coax into fullness. When the promise of these things appears false to an unbelieving generation, then art itself is experienced as a lie. But these things in art, these heartbeats of another life beyond, are anything but man-made. This is why it is only right to be sensitive to their witness, which is that the official story of modern secularism is very far from the truth.

PART II

THE SPIRITUAL DYNAMICS OF ART

In Part I, we tried to get a sense of art as involved, quite 'naturally', in the 'real world'; but we also saw it as involved in decisions and commit - ments as to what the real world is. The making of such choices is a perfectly healthy aspect of the adult life of human creatures, who are not born knowing everything. This aspect of art is the inheritance of Creation, still discernible, still there.

But we also began to see that art now operates under different conditions to those that, at least theoretically, existed in Creation; there is now no flow of innocent attention in our relationships with God or nature; real perception of either is at best intermittent, and at worst distorted by self-regarding bias. This condition not surprisingly affects the ease and delight of doing art; but it has also affected the nature of art.

In Part II, we will be looking at the way an art alternative to 'natural art' has developed, which, far from being an instrument for the mediation of reality, has become more like a tool, a sophisticated one, for conversion towards unreality. Here the term 'conscious and unconscious' do not quite apply, because in religion, you can know what you are doing and not know it at the same time. But then religion is not the consumer choice we think it is: we do not choose; we have chosen, there is no box to tick for opting out.

Oddly enough (but not so oddly if you consider that separation from God has affected all relationships) the assumption that art can connect with reality is by no means universal. The concept of 'truth in art' has become self-conscious and awkward, as if we have lost the right terms to discuss such a notion. So we need to find the implicit, 'natural', connec - tions. This process will then enable us to understand the dynamics of the 'spiritual engineering' in the alternative art that was developed, especially in pre-Christian societies, before coming up to date, and closer to home, in a chapter called 'Personal Spiritual Dynamics'.

Chapter Four

What is an Idol?

Nature is a contested area in our relationship with God. But we have grown used to thinking of it, like our back-garden, as something we simply own, and which we can see as we please; so to call it a contested area sounds at first alarmist and religiously hysterical.

But that is so only if the God-question is left out, and there is no panic on. But if the main issue of existence is not our comfort in this life, but a boardroom battle for the running of the universe, then we are intensely involved in a squabble for every part of the property, in which our ability to define it becomes a tactic in our negotiations.

A brief scene in a television crime drama [9] may help to bring to life the issues we are dealing with. You will need to imagine it with me. In our view, we watch a detective drive up to a fine Georgian country mansion (representing tradition and old family values); this turns out to be the home and office of a supermarket magnate (representing modernity and efficiency). When we enter the building and meet the man, a third element appears: artistic stylishness. Not the conventional businessman, he surprises us by being a modernized aristocrat, long-haired, with a lithe physique like a pop star; and his office is a spacious, pillared hall, walled with bold abstract paintings. Here we have, then, a man who seems to exemplify three 'good' sets of values: tradition, modernity, and art. However, inside his fashionable, but hermetic world, the pop-baronet is found to be making business plans with complete disregard for honesty, indeed for human life. What is odd is that the colourful abstracts which dominate the room are not just a shocking background for his activities (because patronizing the arts suggests social virtue) but also weirdly appropriate. In what lies the appropriateness?

Whoever chose this inspired set was clearly not implying anything as crude as an influence of the paintings on the man's behaviour. It was more an intuited poetic symbolism. Since this art-walled office was the man's world, where he took his decisions, it could also be considered the self-chosen landscape of his mind, the scenery he allowed to look in on him.

---

[9] *A Touch of Frost*, ITV, February 9, 1997.

To get a sense of its atmosphere, it is worth thinking first what it was not. There was nothing 'given' about this interior environment. It mirrored only the man's choice, and not of a specific world, with its own boundaries and obligations (as would the stately home paintings of landscapes, houses and pets we might have expected to see) but an entirely abstract world, into which he could read what he chose. There were not even some ancestral portraits, to remind him of a place in which he was a mere steward among the generations and must give account. All he had to think of was the identity he had chosen for himself, perhaps a fashion he was drawn to. The only break in this insulated world was the view through the windows behind him, silently evoking the order of creation of which he had been made a part; and the knowledge that he was a creature among creatures, owing responsibility. But inside his self-created world, he could feel free to make his own rules, and to forget that the real world would eventually catch up with him.

Many modern offices convey a sense of isolation from the world, just as much as, electronically, they are connected to it. But there is also something about the abstract paintings themselves, as opposed to a bare office wall, or a view outside, that we should notice. Though glimpsed only for a few seconds, they seemed to add their own meaning to the story. On the one hand, of course, they were colourful, cheerful, apt modern decoration for an office, with no existential implications! On the other, they had enough resonance with other contemporary work to register, in contrast to the 'missing' landscapes and portraits, as a kind of sensory denial of the world. This does not mean hatred of it. Plenty of representational pictures convey hatred. It is more that abstract images of this type erect a partition between us and the external world, a 'middle wall' of perceptual interference, like the fuzz on a television screen. This fuzz one could associate with various modern words, such as 'relativism', all of which express the lack of belief that we can have certain knowledge of anything, especially in the area of moral absolutes. Another less philosophical, but more recognizable word from the contemporary experience is 'doubt'.

Doubt, and two stories behind it

The concept of 'doubt' is helpful, because it expands some of the paradoxes of the new art. Doubt should be a tool of questioning, as in Descartes' method, but in the modern period it has attained to a semi-permanent state, of neither acceding nor denying. Denial can be tested, it is either true or false, but doubt can act like a dog at a gate, preventing us getting somewhere, without directing us anywhere else. According to such a code of belief, which as a view of reality is as prevalent as beer and coffee in college and art school, external values are a purely personal matter, not because we would not like to know them, but because we cannot know them. The consequence for the artist, which is not categorically stated, but follows logically, is that she directs totally, and does not have to follow anything external to herself, because none of those things are really real. This is where the 'freedom' of the artist, and the 'freedom' of the business tycoon, begin to connect.

The philosophical story

For our purposes there are two different stories going on here. There is the philosophical story, dating from the Enlightenment attempt to base knowledge on reason rather than revelation, which has had its effects in both social morality and art. In art, the gradual fall-out from eighteenth-century rationalism, reinforced in the nineteenth century as Darwinism helped establish 'naturalism' (i.e. nature is all there is) as the scientific orthodoxy, has *removed the transcendent significance of nature*, and so gradually made representational art seem meaningless, [10] focussing artists more and more inwards on the self, until even that is subjected to doubt. Abstraction appears towards the end of this line, but abstract art is only a small part of this movement. In social behaviour and morality, philosophical develop - ments from Descartes and Kant down to Nietzsche, leading to a belief in the absence of knowable objective constraints in the external world, have made people consciously arbiters of their own moral destiny. A minority of moral experts have helped shore up an ethical consensus, but in general the consequences of the 'death of God' have been as foreseen with such clarity by nineteenth-century seers such as Nietzsche and Dostoyevsky, who realized that at street level, as well as at leader level, it would be hard for morality to survive without meaning.

In the philosophical story, then, there is one stream which has issued in two inevitable consequences: art liberated from objective constraints, and humanity liberated from objective constraints.

However we may suspect that the philosophical story is not the whole truth. It is an account which reads conveniently as a story of victims, in which European civilization, for all its gains in liberty and progress, has been put to much suffering from the unfortunate philosophical mistakes of a handful of bewigged Scottish and French *philosophes*. Indeed, the story is sometimes told as if a catastrophe similar to the Adamic Fall of Man occurred in the eighteenth century, when 'reason' was elevated above revelation, as if the pre-rationalist innocents were doing very well until the Enlightenment snake lured them into intellectual independence. (In

---

[10] The process of the evacuation of the spiritual from nature under the impact of nineteenth-century scepticism, charted dramatically in the biography and thought of Ruskin, is described in Peter Fuller's book *Theoria: Art, and the Absence of Grace*.

any case, those 'innocents' were not doing so well, because 'revelation' itself had been largely captive to a monarchic and church system which had other concerns than the religion of Jesus.) But philosophical trends do not come as an impersonal visitation, independent from the human will.

The underlying religious story

So there is a second story, interwoven with the first. This is a story of people acting on ideas, and also of art acting on people. It is that of a symbiotic relationship between art and behaviour, in which neither is particularly innocent. This story our glamorous magnate also illustrates.

Every monarch needs his props, the wealth and magnificence which convinces him and his subjects of his own glory. But the post-Enlightenment 'monarch', that is, me or you, the newly liberated autonomous individual, also needs his props; to help convince him that he is no longer a creature and that he alone shall rule. His props take the form of an artificial world of cities, of inner chambers which no daylight ever enters, of a mediated world which has neither touch nor smell; and this is reinforced by images which blur that outside world, and bring assurance that nothing in it is really real, or can offer any resistance. Therefore even his most 'spiritual' art, supposedly concerned with the world beyond, may well be designed to reinforce the self, and give no hint that externality means accountability and judgement.

This hints at a bigger role for art than we currently give it. Can it really achieve any of this? It depends on the spiritual energies behind it. On the surface, pictures and works of art are merely commodities owned by the few, and very much at the margins of common life, less important than film or music. But they have their own undisputed territory; from that, and with an enormous following today, they possibly have great power. For if their power of interpreting life, even if only based at the margins, is not disputed, then they exercise a degree of authority over all of life. Such authority is of course 'only' exercised in the mind; but that is the source of decisions and behaviour. A territorial power like this does not require all that many people actually to look at art; it is effective in so far as it is not contested.

Introducing the I-word

The only difficulty in identifying the territorial power of art is that in our society we like images, and we like what they do to us. Their power to control thoughts is even recognized, with perfectly respectable names (advertising is one of them), as society embraces, with all deliberation, the lie. However in the Bible there is only one name for this power, in which image and lie are combined. The word for it is 'idol'. This is a different side to the history of art and of philosophy. It is the story of human nature, crafting its ideas and its artefacts, with great ingenuity, though with great self-harm also, in defiance of God.

There are always these two stories at work: the supermarket magnate is at once victim, deceived into a deathly world of self, and villain, maintaining the lie and trapping others. The artist and art-lover are in the same position, both led and leading. Only God can sort out how these relationships work, and where responsibility lies.

But have we not assured ourselves, in Part I, that art is a good creation of God's? How has it ever come into this position, of being not only the victim, but also the villain? This is not a question about representation and abstraction, but about art as such, in all its forms. The explanation, fairly obviously, has to do both with the nature of art as concerned with truth, and with human nature as concerned to avoid it.

Here we encounter an immediate difficulty. We seem to be taking art too seriously. It is not that there are not many serious paintings around; twentieth-century art has perhaps been more 'serious' than that of any other epoch. But our society has nonetheless succeeded in compartmentalizing art, like religion, not in the 'action' side of life, but in the 'leisure' or recreation area. Fundamentals are already established in the 'action' side of life (the priority of economics, for example), and religion and art are a form of recuperative entertainment, to restore us for 'action'. The presumption is that the 'influence' of art stays firmly within the 'leisure' compartment. Therefore what we see is no more to be taken seriously than what we wear.

Whereas when we try to engage with the Bible on the subject of art, we experience something like the embarrassment of a culture clash. It does not seem to recognize our 'leisure' compartment. It is playing what sounds like a different music. (*Switch radio stations! This sounds heavy!*) It takes life so seriously. It cannot be talking about art, can it? Let us listen to a few excerpts:

A workman made it, it is not God –
the prophet Hosea (chapter 8:5)

If your eye causes you to sin, pluck it out –
Jesus (Mark's gospel, 9:47)

The eye is the lamp of the body.
So if your eye is sound, your whole body will be full of light;
but if your eye is not sound, your whole body will be full of darkness.
If then the light in you is darkness, how great is that darkness!
Jesus (Matthew's gospel, 6:22)

This sound is not the soothing anaesthetic provided by the entertainment industry. It is not a music representing entertainment at all, and it certainly is not tuned to customer demand. It occupies a different space to what we think of as art, with its own resonance, and it draws us across to hear notes and combinations of notes that we have never heard before; sounds that, instead of running round the small scales of earth, arch between heaven and hell. It is a sound so clear and articulate that everything else we have heard fades beside it. It tells us that whatever we do in life, not only doing but also seeing, matters intensely.

The temptation, when we think of art, is to think that the Bible's music is *the wrong music*, that someone has brought the wrong music to the concert and is trying to play it in opposition to the melody the rest of the orchestra has agreed to play. The rest of the orchestra only wants to listen to the good music of art, the music of power, attractive power, without responsibility. It does not occur to them that for irresponsibility they have traded significance; that for unaccountability they have gained irrelevance. But those who start to listen to this 'wrong' music find something in its notes, alongside the warnings, that gathers art again to the centre; it is a music that at once diminishes art, and amplifies it out of triviality.

Jesus is not an idol

I am assuming that when we think we understand idolatry, we don't. Though the word is now increasing in currency, it does not mean anything very precise; it is usually something that applies to other people, and it is generally considered a minor spiritual defect, on a par with over-eating or driving too fast. Whereas, if the central orientation of life is meant to be the true God, the usurpation of that place by substitutes matters very much indeed.

A filmstar is said to be an idol. A public idol in that sense is captive to everything we require them to be. They reflect back to us our ideals, and we demand of them that they do nothing beyond what we, the sovereign public, expect. On the other hand Jesus, if we try to think of him outside the context of sermons and church, was nothing like one of the plastic creations of the PR industry. If a 'spin doctor' had followed him around, we should have neither written gospels, nor any gospel. For far from reflecting just what we want, and saying just what we want to hear, Jesus is different; he has comeback, resistance, solid-rock thereness, standing for himself. This may make him sound overbearing; but the non-idol is not that. He forces nothing. His reality is simply there, quenching by its own truth what we send at him of unreality. Jesus does not need to control; he is reality, there to be adjusted to. Those who tried to own him and could not change him, in the end needed to destroy him. It was the only way they could maintain their right to stay as they were. *Idols can live, but God we have to kill.*

Creation not an idol

Creation also is not an idol. *But unlike Jesus Christ, it is not its own interpreter.* In itself it has plenty of resistance; it is made for relationship rather than modelling in our image; it has power to be itself, to come back at us when we presume too far, refusing to be taken for granted. But it has no right of reply. According to our ways of thinking Creation can be made into what we want, worshipped for our needs, or destroyed for our needs.

An illustration might be our love-affair with the tropical island. Gauguin's art captures the languorous heat, the colour, the sensuality of warm seas, the ease of soft sands, the delectation of blooms and brown skin in shade. If this sounds like a travel brochure, that is just the point. The beauty is there, that is not in dispute. That it touches our senses in a profound way may well signal a yearning in us for the rest of Paradise. But when we try to take hold of it on earth, as a commodity and a due, something very quickly goes wrong: including despoliation by tourism.

If we place ourselves at the centre, and insist that the experience conform to our desires, that it enfold us, we have made an idol of nature and will very possibly come away with nothing. Physical rest, beauty, a tan, and a holiday to boast of at work may all help, but they stop frustratingly short of heaven on earth. The idea does not contain the route to the reality. If, on the other hand, we start to see nature as belonging to God's world rather than as our dream-world come to life, we can begin to relate to it in an open, non self-centred way, and perhaps gain more. Gauguin's world is a bewitching one; it claims to be about the completion we may find in nature, but its hidden centre is the fantasy life of the self. It is about us, rather than about it. To find out what that nature was really like, and how it did not meet his need, we have to turn to the biographies; or to penetrate the deep *ennui*, the dissatisfaction in his paintings.

So nature can be idolized, but it is not in itself an idol. As an idol it works better, if we may put it so, when like tropical islands it is far away. But present nature is a different proposition. It has a way of reminding us that we are merely human, that we are vulnerable creatures, not com - pletely in control. We might even not be God. As such, nature is God's own satellite television station, broadcasting primary theological truth, twenty-four hours a day.

The excitement of nature should be, not in offering it rule over our lives, but in the anticipation it gives of something greater. Of course it does not *prove* there is a God. On the contrary, nature is there, among other things, to make the fact of God blindingly obvious. It is that obviousness which shows what a 'darkened understanding' we have, as St Paul put it. This is nothing to do with romantic experiences of nature, visits to the Lake District etc., though they may help. If one considers St Paul's experiences of nature, of sea-storm and desert, which would hardly have encouraged sentimentality, it is the more striking that he writes:

> For what can be known about God is plain . . ., because God has revealed it . . . Ever since the creation of the world his invisible nature, namely his eternal power and deity, has been clearly perceived in the things that have been made. So they [that is, people in general] are without excuse. (Romans 1:19–20, RSV)

It was not a tamed, prettified nature he was writing about, but a nature that can give us trouble. And it is this nature that speaks of the power and the deity, the godness of God, for it is a fact that it gives him no trouble at all.

Nature always mediated – but in whose interests?

Most people would not, however, agree with the apostle ('apostle' means, incidentally, 'messenger', which indicates that St Paul sees himself as interpreting matters from God's side, not as an offer of opinion) that from nature God's existence and his power are obvious. If they were intended to be so, something has gone wrong. The problem is that we do not just have nature. We have mediated nature, nature mediated by Gauguin, by Monet and Cézanne, by economists and agronomists, by developers and anti-developers, by Chinese, Hindu and African religions, and even in their own dry way, by theologians. The actual stuff is there to touch, of course; no one mediates touch, but in the grown-up world where decisions have to be made, priorities allocated, and values decided, nature is subject to philosophy. Primary experience is already coded before it happens.

Another way of saying this is that object (nature) is largely subject to image (concept, philosophy, religion). This is just a fact about perception. We dig and delve with ideas. We find what we expect, sometimes less, and sometimes more. The Americans, looking at the moon, see nature under a strong concept 'mineral wealth'. They may well find what they are looking for. There may be other things about the moon which however, lacking a concept for it, they will miss. Practical concepts, in the absence of public belief in God, have a way of displacing poetic ones.

Now we need to put together the two considerations, both that nature is mediated to us by images and ideas, and that nature is theologically significant, charged with the most important message, save for the gospel itself, that we shall ever hear. God's message through nature is entrusted to ideas. God does have other means at his disposal. Paul was blinded by a light *brighter* than the midday sun; and there is the word of the gospel itself. But the mediation of nature is still critical. *In whose interests is this mediation being managed?* God has no control over it, or at least he is not often consulted. Is it being managed by a world in rebellion against him, concerned precisely to deny his 'eternal power and deity'?

Nature, seen truthfully, leaves no choice but to worship (God). The clouds in the sky and the trees along our streets ring louder bells on a Sunday morning, so to speak, than any church; but they are ignored from that point of view because worship puts humanity to inconvenience. Worship is the opposite to the lie of self-sufficiency we are leading. So instead of seeing nature as pointing to God, we image it a way that centres it in ourselves.

When St Paul was writing to the Romans he was describing direct idolatry, but the way he puts it also explains indirect idolatry, and makes them both seem equally grotesque:

> So they are without excuse; for although they knew God they did not honour him as God or give thanks to him, but they became futile in their thinking and their senseless minds were darkened. Claiming to be wise, they became fools, and exchanged the glory of the immortal God for images resembling mortal man or birds or animals or reptiles (Romans 1:20–23).

In other words, they scaled down God, by deceptive images, to be more their own size, moulding nature to be less offensively pointing to God. The point about an animal, or a Roman emperor, dressed up as a deity, is not that any real worship of them could seriously be sustained as they are in themselves. They get their spiritual charge, the lust to give them worship, from what they are not being allowed to say about God. The divinized reptile is not exactly a convincing candidate for deity, but he is allowed to be so as a protest vote against acknowledging God. But why the image? Because the image is always more malleable than the object; the real emperor, bird, animal or reptile might not appear so divine. The image loses all the otherness of God, and the otherness of nature as well.

Romantic landscapes and Roman portraits

The statues St Paul had in mind were art only incidentally, of course, but as depictions of nature they also get us to art generally. We could experiment by jumping from St Paul to the Romantic landscape of the nineteenth century. The questions we would ask are similar.

Whose landscape is it? Is it seen open-endedly as God's nature? Or have we domesticated it, or even divinized it? We can enjoy it without asking such suspicious questions, but alongside the observation and love of nature, there may well be implicit spiritual agendas. For example, Turner is reputed to have said, on his deathbed, 'the sun is god', [11] having painted the sun over years as an ungovernable force, the origin and dissolution of life. Well, is it? In the perspective of the cosmos, the sun is a very minor potentate. Many artists have depicted sunlight with great

See Plate 7

---

[11] *Turner*, Tate Gallery, 1974, p. 16.

See
Plate
8
beauty, and attention to its symbolic power, but without any sense of its being other than created. (I have in my mind's eye Dürer, Rubens, Claude, but there are countless others.)

But if the sun is depicted as a power that is subject to no one, a suggestion that in Turner's art is modified by his real devotion to natural truth, then that is simultaneously a statement about it, (an unlimited natural power) and a statement about us (if the sun is not subject, neither are we).

The true idol is the god you can use, or, as the Hebrew prophets said, an idol is a god you can carry about (Isaiah 45:20; Jeremiah 10:5). If Romantic nature is treated by us as a great power, that is in part only to disguise the use we make of it. The early Romantics made much of its sublime, unpredictable force, giving it an almost magical authority. But the actual effect of this endowment is not to diminish humanity, even though it may make you feel 'small', any more than a night at the horror-movies diminishes you; your pleasant *frisson* of fear only tells you that there is no moral power in the universe. If there is no moral authority beyond the moonlit clouds, the squall-thrashed oaks and other dramatic properties of the Romantic vision, then there is none at all, and who is god then? We are.

Idols, then, have the dubious power to attract worship which is in fact disguised self-worship. Even emperor worship, (or more recently, dicta - tor worship), though intensely limiting in terms of personal freedom, essentially divinized the individual. Subsumed within the amoral freedom of the ruling despot, the individuals worshipping him enjoyed, if they could suppress their consciences, complete freedom: from God. They could come into a collective religious belief (which, admittedly had one main beneficiary in this life) that the individual shall rule, and so affirm their own belief in themselves. No doubt the hero-worship of pop stars, where 'image' (though not of stone) is equally important, offers similar spiritual paybacks.

It is not, therefore, as important to distinguish between the use of art in direct idolatry, and the use of art in 'normal' depictions of nature, as we may have thought. In both cases, nature is being made into an image. In the first case, the kind of idolatry St Paul saw, the image is not intended as a window onto nature, but creates an idea, which is seen over and against nature. The statue of Augustus does not introduce you intimately to Augustus, but presents an ideal which, it is hoped, will captivate your mind, even should you meet the rather less perfect prototype. The statue of 'god' Apollo may represent even more of an ideal, of power, graceful beauty and perfection: good things, but not essentially 'other' to the human project, in the way that Jesus is.

See
Plate
9

See
Plates
10 & 11
For the second case, of 'normal' depictions of nature, we could take the parallel example of Roman domestic portraiture. In this, which is much freer to depart from the ideal, an image is also being made, but

outside any religious context. This is, supposedly, neutral art. But if nature was made by God, including human nature, partly to promote understanding of him and worship, any images made of it will have at least some implicit recognition of him, or some denial of him. And if the human form is made 'in the image of God' (remembering that a particular physical form has been chosen by God to bear whatever 'likeness' it is that we have), then any representation will express acceptance, rejection, or blindness to that in us which is reminiscent of God.

Such acceptance can occur without any consciousness of its relating to a 'religious' perception. This may be why, like islands of religious freedom, the lively portrait heads of the Romans were able to appear so unexpectedly in the sea of idealized sculpture, and are so exciting in their humanity and attention to character. They throw some light on what St Paul means by 'holding the truth in unrighteousness' (see Romans 1:18), which suggests that he saw people having the truth in their hands, but not seeing through to its implications.

Of course in the West we have a habit of taking 'realism' for granted, thinking of it as neutral, with little idea of how implicated it is in philosophical and religious commitments. For hundreds of years our Western vision has been informed by Christian ideas, and so our 'neu - trality' is already heavily impregnated with a sense of significance. One has only to compare English landscape painting to Japanese, to see how even Turner's art (which one might normally contrast with that of a professed Christian such as Constable) is deeply founded in Christian realism.

The avoidance of art: a safety zone?

If art does not exist in any neutral zone, but it inevitably takes sides, would it not be best to do without it? The Puritans, those pioneering Christian disciples of the seventeenth century, made a move in that direction by refusing to attend the theatre, a vigorous, if frequently ribald, art form of their time which they felt they could simply exclude. They did not necessarily exclude the other arts, such as music and literature, but the fact was that they were able, in good conscience, to exclude one art. [12] Such an attitude has contributed to the way that art today is departmen - talized, and many well-informed people appear to be able to live without it. For many Christians, the vision of normal, complete Christian living is imagined as if art did not exist. Surely that is not mere philistinism, but an instinctive practical response to an area that at best is too charged with significance.

---

[12] See Leyland Ryken, *Work and Leisure*, pp. 104, 109.

But at this point, we may find ourselves making a large mistake. We conceive to ourselves that there is perception (on the one hand), neutral, scientific, and in our hands sufficiently reliable, and on the other hand there is art, questionable, subjective, and now, we learn, potentially idolatrous. We would naturally, if faced with that alternative, prefer to stay with our 'neutral' perception. But suppose that the nature we *see* is art-mediated, and that we cannot fully stand outside the perceptual free-for-all in which artists, alongside others, engage.

Now of course I am sure that my own perception is art-mediated. I see the world differently because I have seen Constable and Monet, and because sometimes I take up pencil and brush. But perhaps the question goes further than that. Some would argue that there is no other perception than one that has been progressively 'discovered' by artists. The difficulty is, that one cannot see through others' eyes, especially through the eyes of those friends who have not had such an immersion in art, and see what their perception is like.

One influential proponent of the idea of perception as mediated has been the art-historian and psychologist of the arts, Sir Ernst Gombrich, who argued in a famous book, *Art and Illusion*, that each development in the progress of representation in the history of Western art was like the development of scientific theory, which actually changes the general way of looking at the world. This can be seen in reverse, so to speak. Before Constable and Monet, their ways of seeing nature, that we now take for granted, though they were 'there', had no more entered people's heads than had the Theory of Relativity. Those kinds of perceptions were simply a blank screen. Gombrich's theory may suffer too much from the defect of boxing people in, in imagined states of ignorance, when what was really lacking was attention. There is much **See Plate 12** that the artists of earlier centuries did not do, not because they could not see it, but because of their symbolic preoccupations. Dürer's *St Jerome* in the National Gallery shows him painting with 'medieval' detail **See Plate 13** on one side of the panel, and with Turnerian freedom (even spattering paint) as he imagines a fiery star on the other. The institution of art might set practical limits on what he did, but there are no signs of its setting great limits on his perceptions.

At least Gombrich helped us to see that perceptually, there has never been the 'choice' that we experience in the art gallery. Raphael never decided not to paint like Toulouse-Lautrec. There were limits to what he could do. And we can see the world in terms of this year's art, this year's fashions, but not next year's. There are perceptions that have been opened, and some (presumably) that are as yet closed. To this extent, the way the public sees the world has been conditioned by art. Whistler summarized this idea in his epigram 'Nature follows art.' Therefore we cannot cut ourselves off from art. Art chases us into the recesses of our understanding and helps position us in the world.

Some might feel discouraged to think we might be condemned to live in an art-mediated reality, with no escape. Their nightmare might be of being shut up permanently in one of those art galleries that have no windows, and where even daylight from the roof has had to be processed to eliminate anything so much as a gleam of sunlight. Is there no 'exit to reality' (as the philosopher Richard Wollheim [13] has put it, in a critique of Gombrich's book) except what can be seen through the eye of the artist? The truth is, that even the artist needs an exit to reality apart from through art, or art itself would never be modified or developed.

But how are we to understand the perception of the person who is not art-taught? The mistake here is to think of such perception as neutral. *A more correct term might be 'unenriched'.* For art can, as well as deviating from reality, actually lead us to it. An art-mediated reality can, dare we say it, actually improve on what 'normal' perception has to offer, because normal perception may show us very little. The portrait painter, or the person who has looked at portraits, will see what is going on in people's faces in a way that others may completely miss. Normal perception can in fact be a kind of perceptual fog without art.

There is nothing wrong with sight. A dog can find a stick or a biscuit easily by the powers of sight. But there are things beyond being able to find our way across the road, (or being able to read the investment columns in the newspaper), to which we need to be sensitized. They may not seem strictly necessary, but they do help us live above the level of a dog or cat. They are, in other words, not essential to eating, sleeping and mating, but they are essential to the given human programme, which in every settled society has risen beyond these.

Art is positioned in the perceptual area by which we freely negotiate with reality, and find out where and who we are, beyond the needs of dog and cat. This kind of perception, to which there is no equivalent route by other means, though other knowledge may confirm or deny it, will be informed by bad art, by good art, and sometimes by true art. The important matter, then, is not whether to have art, because that seems inevitable at some level, but how we shall have it. This depends on us, but at a deeper level than filtering out bad art through quality control. It is easy to throw down idols – those of a previous generation. But plenty more will spring up, if we want to see the world that way. Far better to make art in such a way that it is not idolatrous at all, but sees reality as it is.

* * *

'Seeing reality *as it is*' is the kind of phrase to which one is unselfconsciously drawn by the very thrust of art. What else is the painter or poet bending

---

[13] Richard Wollheim, 'Art and Illusion', *British Journal of Aesthetics*, III (1963), pp. 15–37.

all her energies to do, than to try to discover and tell the truth about the world? Artists are not there, for the most part, to deliberately lie or steal. They lay out their lives for reality. They care desperately to get across what the world seems to them to be like, and will face enormous opposition to do so. So there is no immediate difficulty with trying to engage with Goya, or Rothko, or Hockney, on the basis of a common desire to know the world as it is. But there are, it hardly needs to be said, enormous problems with the concept. Every one of us in our generation has been taught to see such a phrase labelled all over with 'Handle with Care', or 'Do not Handle at All'. Who, we ask, is the privileged person who has the capacity to know 'reality as it is', and so decide whether the artist has reached the goal? And if art is so potentially idolatrous, what special exemption enables the viewer to be free of idolatry, and to know when truth has been reached or breached? Or if the artist is so likely to get reality wrong, who are we to think we know how to get it right; and if we are right, have we any means of knowing it?

Such questions mainly fall under the heading of 'if we think we know, how do we know that we know?', and have had the effect of undermining the whole confidence of art as a point of contact with the world. We are caught between the over-confidence of science, that there is no intrinsic difficulty about discovery, except funding enough of it, and the under-confidence of postmodernist philosophy, in which real knowledge is a shifting mirage in the desert. Neither are good for art, for the first reduces truth to fact, and the second collapses it to fantasy. Neither view rewards effort in art, because they make truth either banal or inaccessible.

Fortunately, there is plenty of contemporary art that is not intimidated by such philosophy. This is for the simple reason that the inner structure of art itself, its created character which any artist must encounter, tells a different story. The process carries its own conviction. It would be useless trying to stem the flow of a telephone conversation by casting doubt on whether such a technical process could possibly work. The other speaker would know he was connecting with you, and still carry on! Similarly, the normality of art is to make connections; immediacy comes before explanation.

But doubt is corrosive, particularly over the long term. An activity cannot continue indefinitely on impulse and instinct, if its public justifi - cation is removed. For the health of art, we need to understand how its dignity as a propellant of perception can be sustained. And if we are making a case about idolatry, we need to know how to think of art in relationship to that truth, of which idolatry is only the counterfeit.

In doing so, it might be thought I am dragging the reader into the muddy trenches of a long philosophical conflict, in which few of us have any chance of survival, let alone of victory. There are many capable writers willing to do that for you, if you wish! But my object here is to pursue an escape route which has mainly been charted by others, and which begins with the simple premise; that if human life was created by a good God, and he pronounced it good, then there is even an epistemology (theory of knowledge) that is workable, and which does not cause every creative department of life to seize up.

Chapter Five

Relationship of Art with Truth

Truth is something more than fact; which is why artists take so much trouble over it. It is something like 'perceived fact', that which changes you. But it is a problem in philosophy; which is why philosophers take so much trouble over it. That is their trouble; our trouble, as artists, is not in understanding how truth works, but in getting enough of it. It helps, however, to believe it does work.

Art as a form of attention

It is fairly straightforward to see art as something that is directed outside the self, towards something else. This is so whether we think of art as representation, in which case the artist's attention is towards the world or theme being depicted, or of art as invention, in which case the artist's attention is towards the object being realized. Both what Gombrich terms 'matching' and 'making' are activities in which the world external to the self is engaged with.

Imagine two artists from different epochs working side by side: one, the objectivist, is wrestling to realize some aspect of nature. That is a clear form of attention. Monet is exhausting himself with the colour of setting sun on waterlilies. The other, the subjectivist, who has been transported back in time from the New York of the sixties, is the purest exponent of gestural painting. With his eyes shut he covers the canvas with random marks. But even he has to decide when to stop, based on what has been done, and will eventually have an external object to deal with. It will not necessarily have any aesthetic form. But it is still a product, external to the self which produced it. Even as random gestures, it would not be identical to the self, but would be representative of a decision of the self. Therefore something about the object as object would have been attended to. Both Monet and the New York School abstractionist are in an 'I-it' relationship.

There are two points that have to be made about the process of being turned outwards towards something else. The first is that, however unreliable such attention may turn out to be, attention is still attention. The process may be badly performed, but that is what the process is. The second point is that attention is different from proof. Attending to something, and proving that you have done so, are entirely separate operations. Knowing something is a form of attention, and trying to know that you know is actually a distraction from that attention. We need to look at these points in more detail, because they mark the route out of the quagmire.

Attention as an unreliable process

There is a longstanding suspicion of claims to perception. But even in a court of law, where suspicion reaches levels undreamt of even in French postmodern philosophy, it does not follow that because some witnesses tell lies, or imagine things, all do so. The fact that there is bias in the artist's viewpoint does not mean that nothing the artist has to say has any relation with truth, or that the process of truthtelling itself is unsatisfactory. There could, as we have said, be possibility without performance.

The artist John Constable, who thought deeply about how to relate to the Creation, sees the issue not as a structural problem, of whether contact with the real world can be made, but as a moral one, of why such contact is not made more often. In fact, he is not too surprised morally, because he understands such difficulties as due to the fall of our human nature. That knowledge has a moral component is hardly an unexpected idea. It is obvious that the kind of insight with which we are concerned in the arts requires honesty, at least in that area, to attain it. It is obvious too that perception of truth only happens when a person is willing to accept the cost of whatever responsibility the truth brings upon her. And it is obvious that we are not truth-telling creatures, at least not easily to our own disadvantage. The question is not whether my perception works, but whether I work my perception. As Constable so beautifully expresses it:

> We are no doubt placed in a paradise here if we choose to make it such. All of us must have felt ourselves in the same place and situation as that of our first parent, when on opening his eyes the beauty and magnificence of external nature and the material world broke on his astonished sight intensely, with this difference: he was created at once in a perfect state, in full possession of all knowledge and mental perfection, could even call things by their names, and know what it was he saw. The gradual perception of these things to us in our less perfect state, makes them have less effect on us, but it ought not. [14]

Constable leaves aside the question as to whether the world itself is in a less perfect state than it was, to point out that perceptual dullness is a

---

[14] *Discourses*, p. 73.

consequence of spiritual barriers. In that little phrase 'but it ought not', he signifies that humankind in its redeemed state should have those full powers of perception restored.

The process of attention, then, is good, but the manner of applying it may not be. A very different conclusion has been drawn by postmodern philosophy, that the process itself is faulty and necessarily biased. But that view, as is well known, fails through incoherence: it ends up doubting itself. It is of course a powerful polemical tool to suspect everybody; to say that Titian can only see 'as a man', and Artemisia Gentileschi can only see as 'a woman', and Rubens can only paint 'as a Catholic', and Claude can only paint as 'a pastrycook' and so on. It is a tool that is remarkably easy to use, because it does not allow of any legitimate defence. It is like the show trials of Marxist Russia or China under Mao, where someone only had to have a distant relative defined as in the wrong social class, to be 'guilty' of having deviant opinions – who you were was supposed to define what you thought. None of us is in any doubt that there is some truth in this. But of course the criteria for truth have to come from somewhere. Someone always claims to know where the truth lies, and to be able to evaluate bias. There can be no such thing as bias if there is no truth; there certainly cannot be perception of bias with no access to truth.

Despite the incoherence of his arguments, the postmodern bully is a familiar character in the art-critical playground, always ready to react to statements of value with the reply 'that's completely subjective' (as if subjective reactions could tell us nothing about the world) or 'you are only saying that because . . .' (as if a person's bias necessarily affected the truth of their argument). It is hard not to see such loud-mouthed attacks as a form of pre-emptive defence for his own position, which is the assertion that there are no external criteria of value – a belief that is a much-prized source of personal 'freedom'.

Attention as an unprovable process

So far we have argued that the artist can have a relationship with reality by attending to it, but she will have to attend to it very well. There are moral-perceptual obstacles to overcome, but, with Constable, we may believe that true vision of the world is at least theoretically possible. However, that is very far from satisfying criteria of proof that she has done so, or of being able to be in a position to declare infallibly that she has done so. This state of affairs has seemed to many to rule out the idea of contact with reality as having any meaning.

However, the kind of knowing that we are involved with in art, far from needing proof, is almost antithetical to proof. This is for the reason, mentioned above, that knowing (like an artist knowing the feeling and form of a person) is a form of attention directed *to the object*, of total absorption with it; whereas proof is a kind of attention directed, albeit temporarily, *away from the object* to satisfy external criteria. The best parallel is that of relationship. Knowing someone is a different kind of activity and experience from trying to prove you know someone.

With art it is also legitimate to talk about relationship. The relationship of artist with subject-matter will never have the mutuality of person-to-person, but neither is it merely one-way. There is the impress of the thing known on the person knowing. When Hockney, following Van Gogh, paints sunflowers, there would be little point unless the flowers were making their own deep impact on him; Courbet's rocks have affected Courbet, and Monet's waterlilies, as he has meditated on them, have extended him beyond himself as a person.

There is a directness about knowing that is essentially a gift. As with other kinds of gift, it detracts from it to doubt whether it is genuine. To doubt knowing, as such, is immediately to come out of knowing into non-knowing; it does not necessarily improve knowing. The ability to know is a gift that makes human life possible; without some measure of trust nothing works, neither business, government or family life. Even in that most untrustworthy and topsy-turvy community, Stalin's Russia, the business of life had to be managed along networks of trust – such as learning to decode the newspapers, learning which lies meant what truth. Knowing has continually to proceed when proof is not available: which is where the artist comes in. An artist, essentially, invites you into the directness of his knowing, and puts you in a position to share it. The idea of proving that he knows what he knows is quite outside this experience.

Knowing as relational commitment

At this point, especially when we might show our captivity to the 'subjective-objective' divide by wondering 'isn't this model of knowing very subjective?', we need to remind ourselves that knowledge of this sort is intensely object-centred, but in a relational way. 'Relationship' has become rather a pallid word, often meaning these days the exact opposite of commitment, but a relationship that binds with ties of mutual trust is the type of knowing we have in mind. This is entirely consistent with the Bible's 'knowing', a concept which stretches without a break from the master-type of sexual union ('Now Adam knew Eve his wife, and she conceived') down to St Paul's 'Now I know in part; then I shall know fully, even as I am fully known' (1 Corinthians 13:12). A dictionary of Greek words tells us 'in the N.T. *ginosko*, know, frequently indicates a relation between the person knowing and the object known', and describes St Paul's phrase about knowing fully and being fully known as a knowledge 'which perfectly unites the subject with the object'. [15]

---

[15] Vine W.E., *Dictionary of New Testament Words*, pp. 298, 299.

Knowledge is therefore to be seen as something on the inside, rather than an external possession, which can be held without commitment.

Such a view of knowledge completely reverses some of the ways we have learnt to think about art. There has been an expectation that truth in art would be to do with fact. The results of this view are often disappointing in terms of art. 'Photographic' or realistic painting may be accurate in terms of fact, but lacks truth in that it has not engaged personally with what is represented. The work may have cost much in time and effort, but little in terms of the cost of that vision where you allow what you see to change you. Truth arises where there is that readiness for commitment; where in a sense the artist has 'bound' himself to what he is painting. In modern terms, the former, photographic method is very 'objective', and the latter, personally felt method very 'subjective'. But in the Bible's terminology of knowing, the former is not knowing at all, because there is no engagement. The 'subjective' person is the one who has stayed within their own shell, treating the world at arm's length, and the 'objective' one is the person who has shown what usually seems an immoderate devotion to the object. Indeed, when you look at a Van Eyck or a Vermeer, the subjective-objective categories break down: the presence of the artist is the guarantee of the presence of the object.

Guarantee: does that not sound again like the quest for proof? That there is an appropriate kind of assurance in knowledge, which is different again from certainty, is a matter we need to turn to in a moment. As with a Van Eyck, whose *Amolfini Marriage* makes an excellent illustration of the idea, it has something to do with the presence of a witness ('Van Eyck was here' is inscribed in Latin on the painting, just as he is seen in the mirror). First, however, it is important to understand the source of our lust for certainty.

See
Plate
14

Protecting your back: 'Enlightenment' models of knowing

One objection we might have, instinctively, to the model of knowing-as-relationship that we have described, is that it is both exposed and vulnerable. Knowledge, in this way of thinking, is a public statement of who we are and what we are committed to. In an embrace, you cannot protect your back. Your being, as turned towards someone else, is publicly exposed. In a wedding, you declare before all comers that you give worth to the one you are marrying, and that is a statement about both of you, of who you are and what you believe the other to be, a 'public secret' which is vulnerable to attack by any who do not share the same commitment. In a painting, you the artist declare your days-long devotion to a bowl of fruit. You convey knowledge that has come from this long engagement with 'the other'. But the confidence of your knowledge may run out if it is not supported from behind; what you observe and your conviction about it might have to run the gauntlet of every insidious doubt before it attains to 'public truth'. Cézanne's devotion to his apples took a long time to be recognized as publicly significant.

The hidden knower

The model of knowledge we have grown up with is very different from this. It protects its back. It has no exposure. The former kind of knowledge, knowledge as relationship, goes off and does something. It cannot help but be engaged. But the 'Enlightenment' model of knowledge is more de - tached. It might best be symbolized by a solitary individual at a computer terminal, connected to the Internet. Theoretically, he might have access to information about everything. He could find out anything, but nothing sees him. He could possess knowledge, but it would not necessarily possess him. He could own knowledge, like so many encyclopaedias, and simul - taneously be free of it. The 'Web' is an appropriate metaphor for this kind of knowing, because, seated at the centre, there is no need to protect one's back; you remain entirely in control, and operate without any public commitment whatever. The ideal here is to 'know fully' without being 'fully known'. But is this really knowledge?

One may attribute such a detached model of knowing to its source in the Enlightenment, in the project of Descartes to develop an account of certain knowledge: even of certain knowledge of God. Descartes' model of knowledge was based on mathematics, a kind of knowing which it appears possible to manipulate in a detached manner; though that rather disguises the fact that its meaning and point is very much bound up with persons. Its objectivity has an obvious practical appeal: but how was it that this one branch of knowledge became authoritative as the model for all knowledge? Perhaps we need to look at the religious and spiritual, as well as the practical energies involved.

The attraction of certainty

Certain knowledge has many attractions. Being in control, not having to trust, having independent access to knowledge, not being exposed to doubt, all seem useful things in an existence that is precarious and hazardous. To a large extent, certainty is the drive for safety. But safety and relationship do not go together, except through trust. (Even astro - nauts, though they entrust their safety ostensibly to equations, in practice are trusting people to apply them.) Relationship permits things to happen to you. Being born permits things to happen to you, and that is just the beginning! The ideal of perfect certainty is at root a refusal, and a denial, of the fact that we are creatures. To be sure we do have areas we control. Everyone of us has parts of life we understand and are responsible for. But to a large measure, we have to exist in trust.

The ideal of certainty puts the human creature at the centre, a little 'god' knowing everything, though in fact deprived of relationship, having only a surface knowledge of things. Trust, however, enables us to place God at the centre, knowing only what we need to know, and thereby being freed of a great deal of responsibility, to concentrate on the relationships he has given us.

Given the apparent possibilities of infinite knowledge, temptingly laid out before us on the Web like so many 'kingdoms of the world', it does seem recklessly extravagant to pour ourselves out in artistic attention on a single piece of fruit, or in devotion towards a sole individual; but in trust that the management of the universe is God's, we are freed to concentrate on what we have been given to do. 'Thy kingdom come, thy will be done, on earth as it is in heaven' can in fact only be brought about by an aggregation of such faithful, local acts of love, in which the power of heaven is willingly focussed, for a time, on a very minute area: which can be done, if the orchestration and outcome of these sometimes unlikely acts is left to God.

Valid assurance of knowledge

However, having an ideal of knowledge that is not based on certainty raises another question of trust. How do we remain open to the true prophet in art, the one who has something new and genuine to say, and defend ourselves from the false prophet, the one who claims to know, but whose work is not true at all? Are there effectual criteria outside those of certain knowledge?

Discerning reality

In practice we operate such criteria all the time. Walking down a stone passage in Warwick Castle, now owned by those masters of illusion, Madame Tussauds, I happened to notice that some of the 'stone' looked odd, tapped it and found it to be hollow. Real stonework had merged imperceptibly with false. It is the same with the boundaries of reality, disclosed by art. Some of them sound hard as you tap them, others ring hollow. At a passing glance, much of it may look genuine, but with attention and engagement you find the truth.

As with stone, one of the main criteria you look for is *resistance*. You want to find true externality in the work, to see that it has been carved out of the real world. It is more than just a projection of the artist's own will, but has had a power to impact him, and it is sufficiently different from him and you to impact you. In the Bible, the false prophets told people what they wanted to hear. They could easily manufacture a message to match consumer demand (e.g. 1 Kings 22, Jeremiah 28). Their job was to shield people from reality. The true prophet had suffered the message, had received it at great personal cost from the Reality of realities, and owed entire faithfulness to the reality he had seen, in the teeth of consumer demand. This principle might make public opposition seem the sign of the genuine work. That would be very convenient! But it would excuse us from the personal cost of judging the work itself, whether it measures up to, and introduces us to, reality.

We are, in effect, asking whether the artist has been in genuine relationship with the world, and has brought something back with him. We are asking whether, through the medium of himself, he has got outside himself. Going back to Courbet: because this need is so central to art, it seems somewhat superfluous when an artist calls himself a 'realist'. It makes me look almost suspiciously at his rocks, and nudes, because I wonder whether by an ideology of realism one can really attain to the fullness of reality, which as we have been saying, has a spiritual dimension which the convinced 'realist' might easily miss. If I find too much of the polemicist in Courbet's art, that is not to say that there is not profound pleasure to be had from his tenacious observation and determined fieldwork.

But there is also another criterion of externality which we particularly apply to art (as opposed to prophecy, though prophecy may employ it), which is its use of *form*.

Form as herald of reality

The poet sweats until each word is in place. His medium is sound, rhyme, rhythm and meaning, and he is just as concerned as any plumber that there are no leaks. The painter lies in bed worrying as to how she may be able to reconcile tonally a small area of her painting. The architect is anxious as he sees a whole facade collapsing: visually, not physically, because a proportion is unresolved. These people are preoccupied with form. They are its master and its slave. And what they strive to perfect, any member of the public, without any ability to help, can immediately see the faults in. Form stands over against the artist, their love and their scourge.

Form is, in a sense, an agreed criterion of art, because it is something that both artist and his public accept that he is trying to do. It stands objectively, because based in the object, outside both of them. Agreement over form is the common task of art. But does this make it in any way a criterion of truth?

Form has something in common with reality, in that it is genuinely external to the self. When the artist is struggling with form, his sensitivity is for the relationship of part to part. His personal taste has to submit to the needs of the relationships within the work. So when a work is finished, there will indeed be truth in it, the truth of the relationships that have been perceived and responded to. A master colourist will have seen very exact relationships and honoured them precisely. That is a true response to physical reality.

The created form will also become a part of reality. There is a difference between the artist's palette left around – which may contain an amazing array of harmonious mixtures, but will essentially be the record of an act, the trace of his gestures – and the finished painting, which has been created to stand alone. The painting can rest complete, when its form requires no more attention, and when *the reality in it* is also complete, requiring no additions or further explanation.

The question is, whether there is any connection between the completeness of form, and the completeness of the reality represented in the painting. If there was, complete form would be a criterion of truth. We can all perhaps think of works of art which are formally complete, but lacking in truth, poems which are finely written nonsense, and architecture which obeys the rules but is hardly worth a glance. However, in the true work of art form and content are not so split; that is the point of it, and the artist who tries to push out the boundaries of form does so by taking in more of reality. Even in writing this book, it may be the rhythm of a sentence that compels me to think further into the subject, to complete the line of thought. The obligation of form becomes the excavator of thought. What is almost eerie is when the form starts to provide the thought.

It is strange indeed that there should be such a synergy between form and content. It is true that when a hymn writer asks me to sing about God's 'face', because in a previous line he had meditated on 'grace', I might wonder whether theological truth has been steered by the requirements of form; but very often, such rhymes, far from limiting thought, have actually taken it into new territory, and almost seem to have been 'given' for the purpose. The real poet makes his passion for poetic form the butterfly net by which he captures fleeting experience. Unless the amazing coincidence of form and content that reality provides is accepted, it would be impossible to be a poet; and likewise, the artist must accept the blessing, and not suspect it, when as so often form and content concur.

Form, then, may be a test that an artist is dealing with reality, but it is not an exclusive test. The fact that an artist has been able to separate herself from a work and call it 'finished' requires it to contain both an idea and the full realization of it in form; it has to have, as it were, both person and body. You could, theoretically, produce a body without a spirit (all form and no idea), or a spirit without a body (all idea and no form), but the work of art requires one to animate and realize the other.

It does seem surprising that something as significant as truth should be loaded into the frail vessel of form. One might imagine it should be otherwise, and that truth should never be allowed out of the safety of steel-lined propositions. But God seems to have ordained it that truth should be touched, handled and seen as well as understood; and to have provided a providential richness of circumstance out of which form and content can be found and mixed; (and here is an example of a sentence, needing a certain balance and weight, which I cannot think of anything to say to complete!)

Accountable knowing

The above account of assured knowing may still not leave us very assured. If I look at a picture, for any discernment of truth in it I am entirely thrown back on myself, it seems. It is true I have the realization of form to guide me, and there may be a public recognition of the artist to build trust, but in the end it is up to me to see if I sense sufficient 'resistance' in the work of art to say that it is indeed a perception of the real world, to be attended to. What makes this different from every man dependent on his own opinion, or worse, 'I don't know much about art, but I know what I like'. What makes this form of 'knowledge' any more than subjectivity in disguise?

There is a difference, but it largely depends on explaining something we have hitherto left out. We speak of knowing as if there were two, or at the most three terms we have to deal with. There is self, (subject), the work (object) and the real world, to which the object may or may not refer. The frustration is that we cannot get outside ourselves to arbitrate between object and world. We can only see from our view, or from others' views, in so far as we can believe them. To be sure, the Enlightenment project was to imagine an independent point of knowl - edge, as if from a satellite, above and outside us, but apart from its giving a very dry, flattened kind of knowledge (like satellite pictures), it does not solve the problem which besets us: how to validate what we see. It is the knowledge inside ourselves, not that outside ourselves, which is the problem.

If there are only two terms to knowing, subject and object, existence is indeed bleak. (Descartes foresaw this, and placed 'God' at the centre of his theory of knowledge, but his successors explored the consequences of leaving God out). We cannot get outside the knowing centre. But if the true centre of knowledge is outside ourselves, that is, it is God, then our knowing is no longer alone. In Jesus Christ, the Scripture says, are hid 'all the treasures of wisdom and knowledge' (Colossians 2:3). This means that my relation to the world out there is transformed by the knowledge that there is truth about it, and that the totality of its truth is known. What it is has been grasped, and is in a sense fixed. It has been understood by a being so morally perfect that there is no possibility of distortion in his view. His mind is a perfect mirror of how things actually are, shorn of pretence and pretension. In him truth exists, and nothing can bend or shake it.

It might seem the next step to close the epistemological circle by asking for access to this truth. We wonder why it is 'hid'. But the important point to notice is what happens when we know it is there. If we know that the truth is there, that does something to our truth. And it is our truth that is the issue. Our truth becomes accountable, and is disciplined by the knowledge that the truth really exists, and one day will be disclosed. Reality disciplines us, because we are no longer accountable to ourselves, but have to give account of our understanding to God. That still seems to mainly leave us with two terms, subject and object, with a third term, the adjudication of God, deferred. But the presence of God's truth as a living point of reference in fact transforms all our perceptions, so that they are under discipline and illumination.

St Paul, as we have quoted, wrote 'now we know in part'. He looked forward to the day of full knowledge. This must be a privilege that comes from union with God. But as far as this life was concerned, he was content with the limitations of being a creature. Being a creature is to know enough, but not everything. St Paul had 'an abundance of revelations'; Christ shared so much of his own nature and truth with him; but Paul did not thereby put himself above men. He lived as a man among men, accepting the limitations of place, time, and not knowing the future. Even sharing so much of the truth of God, he was not ashamed to be dependent. It was sufficient for knowledge that he knew the one who knew.

But is this the hard currency of knowing we are looking for? Paul's personal knowledge is far from providing any form of guarantee that what he knows is the truth. It seems so. But it expands outwards in a surprising way. It does not arm him with proofs, but it does make him a witness.

Knowing as witness

Witness has become a weak word, besides 'proof'. But knowing in the world is structured to take account of witness. Witness is vivid, appre - hendible reality, known in the account of a person. Witness is something different from the bare assertion of knowledge, the false prophet's self-proclaimed opinion, which refuses any attempt to get behind it to its source. Witness is an account of reality which someone binds himself to with his life. In art, the integrity of the artist is part of the chain which creates acceptability for the work of art. The life of the artist is behind the painting, which is one factor that makes works of art so precious. We respond to the witness of the artist, and may do so, not with proof or arguments, though they may be included, but with our own public commitment. We publicly stand where the artist stands.

This kind of knowing, therefore, far from operating in a detached manner, works in a chain of responsibility. We see only from our small corner, aided by those universal truths we are given. But we do know enough to give account. If we can account for it before God, we can account for it in public. Of course we cannot stand outside our own truth, to have certainty. But if we have to make choices, we know enough to choose. And if we have chosen, that becomes a fact about us, and we are able to stand – if we have the courage.

We are back to the picture of knowledge as relationship. What I claim to know, is something to which I have wholeheartedly turned, of which I can give account. I can give an account for it, because an account will be required of me for it. When I am in the embrace of love and commitment, I cannot step outside it and protect my back. I can only be where I am. I cannot draw you alongside and force you to see what I see. But if I am serious that I see what I see, as well as proclaiming it, I will give account for it with my life. This is not certainty for myself, this is not proof towards others, but it is the logic of knowing. As the early Christians found, the assurance of faith *plus death in the arena* is the best epistemology.

A personal account

I am aware as I write that some people are not at all bothered with these questions, and if they were, St Paul is not the doctor to whom they would go. I was myself a late developer in this respect, and remember thinking at school that 'how do I know what I know?' was among the most futile questions ever asked. But its importance for art was borne in upon me in two ways. First of all, there was the 'Emperor's New Clothes' period of modern architecture, when buildings that were transparently cheap and ugly were springing up everywhere, and yet criticism was forbidden under the injunction 'everything you think you see is a subjective opinion'. It was impossible, mentally, to protest, because there was presumed to be no certain knowledge in aesthetics (which, in the light of what I have said above is true): and this became license for aesthetic murder. There had to be a way out of this prison, into which 'subjectivity' had apparently confined us. It needed to be possible to say things about the non-mathematical world, believing them to be true. Otherwise the powerful could continue to do what was transparently wrong in the name of good.

The second event for me was the realization that not only the critic, but also the artist was in a prison. I had naively thought, perhaps as the child of a landscape painter, that the artist's goal had something to do with reality. What drove him on was a passion to get outside himself to truth, very often the particular truth of a place, a person or a theme. Then I read the Bloomsbury critic and artist Roger Fry, the main promoter of Post-Impressionist art in Britain (he invented the term), and found that in his influential theories he denigrated the particular; for him art had only to do with certain universal emotions produced by form, to which the particulars of subject and content were incidental. I did not believe him; but I began to realize that there was assumed to be a kind of veil between the artist and the real world. It began by considering, with Fry, that visible reality was mere matter-of-fact and unimportant compared to the world of ideas (a very Greek idea); and it continued in other writers with the assertion that the real world is inaccessible anyway. I have already mentioned Gombrich's subtle book, *Art and Illusion*, a book much-discussed in its day, which had perhaps inadvertently, but very influentially, drawn this forbidding conclusion.

From his friendship with Sir Karl Popper, Gombrich had reportedly based his concept on Popper's theory of science. Gombrich put forward the idea that the artist's perception of the world, like a theory in science, is no more than a hypothesis, which could be demolished by the next researcher in the field. Even Constable, an artist around whom much of the book was based, could never have assurance that his perceptual contact with clouds, and trees, and sunlight, was real. Another artist could have turned up (Monet?) and shown him that his perceptions were wrong. But of course (which Gombrich knows perfectly well, which is why his is a subtle, but not a consistent book) Monet does not demolish Constable in the way that Copernicus demolishes Ptolemy, and Kepler demolishes Copernicus, though Monet does alter how we see Constable. In any case, as has been pointed out, Popper's is not a convincing account of science, where there is in fact an abundance of secure knowledge, on which people rely when doing dangerous things like flying to the moon. But however great the inconsistencies in application, what was clear to me from Gombrich was that there is a philosophical problem in explaining how something as ordinary as perception of the world takes place, and that as far as he was concerned, there was no way out. The artist could make a best guess, but he could not get there. The professional philosophers to whom I turned next were little more help. Truth had indeed become a term with little application to art. Art, they were agreed, was not about replication, which was the only truth that could be proved; therefore it could not be about truth. The artist's prison was complete.

These things mattered to me. For a start, the idea of being perceptually imprisoned, and of my perceptions of nature and love having no real meaning, made me very depressed! I might look at a tree, and know that however I felt about it, I had no real contact with it whatever. I might as well be in a glass box. Of course, being all alone in the world did make me feel very important! But it was not a way to go on; it was radically inconsistent with any philosophy that ever had, or as far as I could see, ever would produce good art, and it did not seem to accord with the world in which rich and poor, academics, cooks and cleaners, actually have to exist.

The conclusions I came to, after some fairly radical heart surgery of a spiritual nature, were that much of the basis of the discussion had been simply wrong. (I would add that the 'heart surgery' also brought me into an abundance of help with my philosophical troubles. Readers may recognize my deliverers as the philosopher-scientist Michael Polanyi, and his theological interpreters T.F. Torrance and Lesslie Newbigin, to whose sensitive analysis and timely explanation I owe the debt of a great release.) It became clear that any account of knowing that excluded the knowing of God was certain to be false; if you alienate humans from their maker, you alienate them from the world as well. If one kind of knowing will not work, neither will the other. The ideal of certainty (as Newbigin has so well explained) had become a fetish of the modern age. And 'truth', far from being considered to be the impersonal access of the human creature to facts, in which there might be all kinds of perceptual mishaps, should be seen much more as the moral commitment of the person to an alignment with reality as seen by God. And this should be experienced not so much as a hazard, but as a responsibility, impossible to achieve in its totality, but something that can be practised within the freedom of God's grace. We are both accountable and (mercifully, aware as we are of the great inadequacy of our grasp on truth) accounted for.

The widely-reported divorce between subject and object had, therefore, turned out never to have taken place; and this news re-opened for me the possibility of art, glorious art, which operates in that non-guaranteed world of understanding in which we have to live. With the proviso, that such a divorce might still be taking place in us, if, ignorant of our deliverance, we were still hooked into idolatry.

Chapter Six

The Inadequacy of Idolatry

Idolatry is a form of substance abuse; and it is the effects of the substance, not just the attitudes of the abusers, that we need to look at. Classical art, and tribal art, are potential examples, because they were developed in relation to direct idolatry. Western artists have of course been fascinated by their formal qualities – but perhaps they have been drawn by something more mysterious too. Yet there is another 'substance', also to be found in the artistic tradition, which we will, I hope, find even more attractive; it is something so normal and unassertive, that I am calling it 'small art'.

What art has

One limit to our discussion of the perception of truth, is that, following science, it still seems to see significance as conferred by the artist. That, at first sight, is confirmed by a visit to the art gallery. Anyone visiting a gallery will be continually excited by the power of art to represent, not just things and places, but states of mind and whole ways of being towards the world. The artist seems to live on our behalf, demonstrating a mode of being, lived up to the limit, represented in the whole gesture of his work. But as we move our thinking from 'subjective' to 'per-sonal-objective', we begin to see that there has been another story at work. This has been the artist's ability to see and convey *'inherent significance'*, 'meaning that is there'. This has been, I believe, particularly characteristic of the art of the Christian centuries. But how can we possibly distinguish between 'meaning that is there', and 'meaning that is imposed'?

That we can do so, I believe, is because of signals we pick up about the artist's relationship to the viewer. As we travel down the artistic centuries, we will be aware that the relationship of artist to us and to the world changes. Speaking very generally, the artists of, say, the Renaissance to the nineteenth century communicate to us on the basis of shared experience, whereas in the modern period, we take reality more on trust via the artist's experience. There is more of a sense of the artist as the exclusive gateway to a particular facet of life. To believe it, you need to follow the artist, through his door and into his world, but it is not so clear that you have your own door.

In the earlier kind of art, it is much easier to speak of art as a form of knowledge, even if the knowledge is of spiritual realities that are far outside most people's experience. We can look at Giotto's frescoes of the gentle-spirited St Francis, recognizing in him someone we can 'know' and love, and watch his miracles without any sense that Giotto has taken up his beliefs in a merely personal way. The artist places himself alongside us seeing such scenes not as personal to him, but representing a reality that stands as much outside him as it does us. It is the manner of the artist that gives us some clues about the matter that he has seen.

When we think soberly about this, we cannot (or at least ought not) but come to the conclusion that art has benefited greatly from what Christianity calls 'revelation', which is to say significance which is delivered by Word, externally to us, but which is seen to be inherent in those things to which it refers. Giotto is spiritually informed (by 'revela - tion', which included the 'revelation' to the whole church of Francis' life, which had transformed his significance from that of unwanted outsider to authenticated saint), through which he sees not the bare facts, but the unveiled meaning that is there. Another example would be the famous painting by Ghirlandaio in the Louvre, in which an old man with a bulbous and pockmarked nose is smiling at a child. Within the context of significance and love, which only the gospel can have provided, the disfigured old man is not an object of disgust, or even of pathos. The word of meaning has unlocked the presence of beauty.

See Plate 15

A further instance of *meaning supplying vision*, from later in the Renaissance, could be drawn from a painter who was not known as especially devout, but whose thinking was saturated in Christian (as well as classical) concepts. Titian's portraiture has done much to define his age for us, and it is he who especially was entrusted with the images of kings. We all know, of course, that a king is a human being, like ourselves. But what is the significance of this information, and what should someone portraying a ruler do with it? A theological context is needed, in which such a man is neither deified, nor denigrated. When Titian, who well understood the allurements of Renaissance individu - alism, came to paint his Augsburg portrait of the most powerful European monarch ever, Emperor Charles V (Munich), he painted him as an approachable man in a chair, someone who knew that he was himself a subject, and who had to justify his actions before an eternal throne. It is perhaps the sense that the sitter bears responsibility, alert as one ready to take decisions, which gives us the clue to his position. This readiness of the artist, in an understated way, to explore something like the inner nature of authority, expands our sense of the dimensions of humanity itself: a mortal in space, inhabiting a larger space than the picture's frame.

See Plate 16

'small art'

Such, then, is the excitement of art that it can bring us into a form of knowledge that is a real apprehension by a gifted individual of the way things are. If that is the case, then it gives the artist a real freedom from political or personal agendas. Art that is focused on external meanings, even those discovered through revelation, is strikingly free. It is able to follow understanding wherever it goes; and as it does not have any programme for manipulating the viewer, it can follow truth without looking behind itself to measure its effect. It brings the observer into a free relationship rather than one of control, in which the artist becomes as much the viewer, when the work is finished, as any member of the public. As an artist friend explained it to me: 'I want to produce pictures which are healing, not through me but in themselves, so that when they are finished and I have released them into the public world, they would be able to be healing to me as well.' Instead of standing beside his art like a conjuror, on whom it is totally dependent, he sees himself alongside other members of the audience.

But there is one drawback, if you choose to see it so, to this kind of art. It is 'small art': it cannot act in a completely imposing way, because it reveals its sources. This is the price of being a discoverer of knowledge. You stand beside it rather than in front of it. I saw recently the *St Jerome* by Dürer which the National Gallery has acquired. This is a physically small painting, though that is not what I mean by 'small art'. It compacts into its tiny dimensions an intense loading of natural observation and spiritual awareness. But despite its evident mastery, it is also imbued with what we would immediately sense as a humble spirit, by which I mean that the artist allows you to be transported by his own wonder. The 'what' of what he shows is at least as important as 'who' has shown it. Furthermore, when he paints the saint's face, he allows the look on it of spiritual exaltation to appear so relational that the true subject of the picture very quickly becomes the invisible God. Jerome is in touch with God, worshipping 'in spirit and in truth' (John 4:24), but this is not something that the artist has contrived to expound – it is simply there. Dürer has allowed himself to be not the propagandist of an idea but the vehicle of a whole truth that he has perceived. This is what makes this kind of knowledge 'small art', in that although the range of its truth is so vast, its manner of delivery is so self-effacing. To my mind, truly great art is always 'small art'.

See Plate 12

'What art has', then, in principle, is not only contact with reality, but the substance of knowledge, discovered through an informed under-standing: and this is conveyed, without imposition, but with a sense of shared wonder, to the viewer.

What the idol does not have

From the transparency and humility of art, art of a certain kind, we move to what we might expect will be the opacity and ostentation of the idol. Or are idols themselves trying to be transparent to some perceived external reality? What can we learn from how idols operate, that is, real, functioning works of 'religious technology', to illustrate the meaning of art?

There is of course an unlimited variety in forms of religious images, ranging from the realistic statuary of Greece and Rome, to the bizarre (to Western eyes) imagery of Hinduism, to the fearsome visages of tribal art, and to the thing-culture of Western materialism. What follows is a schematic presentation which does not fit everything equally well (be – cause humans are so perverse they might worship almost anything), but which makes some broad distinctions which are helpful for finding our way in art.

We start with an extraordinary paradox. We have seen that the impulse of the artist is to bring his work to life, to give it an independent existence from himself. He is one who will work until his form has the power to live on its own, and he can release it into the world. You would think that this sounds very like the idol maker. Surely he of all people wants to give his objects 'life' so that they can seem to be endowed with presence and power. But here the idol maker is in a dilemma. Life is an attribute of things in creation. From the lowest to the highest level, life speaks of God, the one who gave substance, form and breath. We have argued that 'natural art', by taking its place in creation, has the power to speak of God. *But the idol maker does not want you to suspect that his 'god' is in fact a creature*; that physically it is no more than a creature of the craftsman who made it (which we are never in any doubt about with art), and that spiritually, the presence who is supposed to work power through it is also a created being, a sorry subject of God and not a god himself.

The idol maker, then, has an interest in not constructing a 'complete' work of art for two reasons. On the one hand, what is wanted is an image to 'contain' some kind of spiritual endowment, to provide its power and spiritual connection; and on the other it must not seem (artistically) too complete, lest that gives away its status as a merely created thing. *Either way, it is likely to be significantly 'lifeless'; it has refused the reflected life of the true work of art, and awaits the endowed life of the invoked spirit*. This helps to explain the paradox in the way the biblical authors describe idols, as simultaneously empty, and as coming under judgement. The images themselves fall short of their pretension, and neither does the power behind them have a future:

> Every goldsmith is put to shame by his idols; for his images are false, and there is no breath in them. They are worthless, a work of delusion; at the time of their punishment they shall perish. (Jeremiah 51:17–18, RSV)

We are able to contrast the idol, then, with art. The idol image is literally soulless and incomplete, as an entity with pretensions to power (it has 'no breath in it'), but that is also true artistically. Its incompleteness is filled externally, by a spiritual power. This could be something attributed by the idolater to give it life, or it could be something formally invited in, as when the 'god' was called on to occupy his image.

Attributive power: from dolls to divinities

The work of art, then, is complete and self-sufficient, but the idol 'lives' by the powers wilfully attributed to it. We can understand from the experience of childhood some of the non-artistic abilities of the human imagination to endow objects with life, when even the least lifelike dolls and bits of rag can have independent life and personality attributed to them. There is nothing magical or idolatrous about these, of course, because children are not praying to them or attempting to extract favours. But they do evoke a power of allegiance which, confronted by their physical appearance, is very difficult for an adult to grasp (!). There is something equally baffling about the attributive power of idolatry. This is illustrated by the paradigmatic Old Testament story of idolatry, that of the Golden Calf, told in Exodus (chapter 32) in which an image, fresh from the foundry, is treated and worshipped as the deity which had just rescued Israel from Egypt. One wonders how convincing an image the calf had to be, or whether, since the desire to make a visible 'God' was there, any image (this reminds me of some church art!) would be welcomed.

This leads us to the insight that the information-content of the idol need not be great. We have characterized the work of art as a form of knowledge, in which the artist allows you to share his knowing. But if the human powers of attributing 'life' to dumb idols are what we believe them to be, the idolatrous work of art does not need to have that power of reference to external reality which so excites us in art. Reality, in fact, is just what it does not need. Its purpose is to attune you directly to a spiritual source which appears to be above and beyond creaturely reality. If by contrast we think back to the Dürer, its information content is high, in that it leads you out and into the physical and spiritual realities which we all share, and which can be tested; rather than offering any private route to an ill-defined spiritual experience.

We need to test out these concepts on some examples, but also to note in passing that if the power of filling in the information gaps from our own will-to-worship is so great, that should cause us to ask ourselves what sort of art we are looking at, whether it has life, or whether it needs wishing into life by us. With any new thing I see, (a new sculpture, for instance, chanced on when visiting a gallery) I have to decide whether to spend time engaging with it, and then, whether it will enlarge my experience and bring me into some truth; or whether some act of complicity is required of me to give it meaning. If that is the case, I will usually end up feeling subservient to its idea, impressed with the artist, but not at all enlarged myself. I have enlarged it, but it has not increased me. That, for me, would be the sign of having been in the presence of something that functioned a little like an idol.

You would think that such a sense of self-abnegation before the work of art was an ordeal to be avoided. But on the contrary, when one reads the literature of art, such as modern art magazines, the language of worship is often so strong that it appears that for many people, the experience I describe is what draws them into art. There is a payback for the worshipper, of course. If much of the experience has been contributed by your own endowing mind, you ultimately have only yourself to thank.

Enlivening the idol by imaginative complicity

If we go back to the prophet Jeremiah's definition of the idol as without breath, we have implied that there are two routes by which that want of 'breath' might be supplied. One route is from the worshipper's imagina-tion. What I have called the 'complicity' of the worshipper is required, in that he will have to involve his mind, usually in the form of a lie, to supply the lack in the work. We are most familiar with this process in advertising, where we willingly play the game of 'Girl + Car' (incomplete and unfathomable statement as it stands) = (our part) 'warm feelings of masculine prowess associated with expensive and dangerous metal toys which will spend a lifetime in traffic jams'. In art it may not be very much more complicated. The Van Dyck portrait may present a similar riddle: 'Idle English landlord dressed up like Catholic saint' (illogical combina-tion), with which we are invited to comply, by concluding the false logic 'birth confers nobility', a gain for the artist in politics, if not in accurate portraiture. But advertising is different from art (and Van Dyck's art is not in his advertising).

See Plate 17

Where this power of supplying the missing logic of art becomes more significant, is where the artist is trying out a philosophy that cannot be completed by natural observation, and must be completed by our own willing suspension of disbelief. Mondrian's abstracts, for example, can-not be understood without at least some attunement on our part to the possibility that his theosophical premise might be right, that there is a world 'in here' which has priority over the world 'out there' (see Chapter 7).

Enlivening the idol by the spirits of the gods

a) The gods of Greece and Rome
The other route of supply, of 'breath' (life) to the idol image, is not so
much from our imaginations as the direct one of invoking spiritual powers
to indwell it and work through it. If that is done, one would not think
the appearance of the image greatly mattered. In fact, the use of the
imagination and the spiritual powers often seem to have worked together.
We could take two divergent examples, the realistic god images of Greece
and Rome, and the terrifying unnaturalistic images found in tribal art.

Robin Lane Fox, the classical scholar, in his *Pagans and Christians*,[16]
tells us that in the ancient world images of gods were often hidden in
temples or covered up, and only revealed for processions and feast days.
Such practices accord with the idea of the image being treated as having
power in itself, aside from its appearance. But he also describes the impact
the sculpted gods had on people's imaginations, entering into their
dream-lives, and defining how they thought of the god. He makes much
of the awesome appearance of two statues recently recovered from the
seabed at Riace, Italy. In this sense, the 'information-content' of the work
of art was, after all, very important. It both gave the god a personality,
and set limits on it. He speculates on the craftsmen who made the statues
being themselves influenced by spiritual powers, by which inspiration
they might bring the 'god' to visible realization.

The Greek and Roman gods are very precise in depiction, and leave
nothing to the imagination. At first sight, therefore, they do not seem to
accord with our schematic understanding of the idol. Robin Lane Fox
however is at pains to point out that real spiritual entities, rather than just
ideas, were considered by both pagans and Christians to be at work in
them, and he sees no reason as an historian to dispute that. St Augustine,
also trying to make sense of the paganism of his day, quotes a pagan author:
'Hermes asserts that the visible and tangible idols are in some way the
bodies of gods; certain spirits have been induced to take up their abode
in them, and they have the power either to do harm, or to satisfy many
of the wants of those who offer them divine honours and obedient
worship . . . He refers to a kind of technique of attaching invisible spirits
to material bodies'.[17] And yet, the statues of the Roman gods are so close
to living, breathing works of art, exercising what power they have
artistically, that there appears to be no 'gap' for the spiritual power, or the
imagination to fill.

However, since we are not dealing with crude mechanics but with
mysterious (or at least devious) powers, we need to look at such statues

---

[16] For the following, see particularly his chapter 4, 'Seeing the Gods'.
[17] *City of God*, Book VIII, Chapter 23, p. 331.

closely, not least by considering their long-term influence in European art. Suppose that someone did want to make 'a god', worthy of worship, worthy of the god's spirit inhabiting it. Suppose they wanted it to be representative of what they considered to be good, for a 'good god', and suppose that the sculpture was itself a work of worship, designed to give praise and honour to the supposed deity. What that craftsman would, given the skill and imagination, come up with would be an ideal, a human-based idea of perfection. This is in fact what the best of the classical sculptures represent, utterly gripping and bewitching ideals, that have been capable of fatal attraction down the centuries, even to the point of seeming to embody an original innocence.[18]

Those who have had first-hand experience of the art of the Greeks will know how potent, how almost overwhelming, their vision of the ideal can be. Even their buildings (I have seen the temples at Paestum, and also at Lindos on Rhodes), without any statuary, can play on every sense, to give a longing to participate in the exaltation of humanity to their perfection. But it is a perfection of nature, and has nothing to do with the generous, self-giving, divine humility of God. Place the marred face of the Christ next to serene Apollo, and we might have an idea which we would rather be, but we would also know which one represented the truth. This battle for the soul between ideal and reality has of course been played out through the history of Western art, especially since the Renaissance, when the church sought to assimilate the mythology and art of the ancients, without being dominated by it.

See Plate 9

Nowhere is the battle more dramatically seen than in the art of Michelangelo. The rediscovered Roman sculpture taught him how to see the human form, and how to idealize it to make it a profound vehicle of thought. But in the battle between Apollo and Christ, there were times when Apollo (the grace of Greek art) won. Howard Hibbard writes of *The Last Judgement*: 'The central figure of Christ, nude and beardless, is like an antique hero-god . . . and has always been recognized as more Hellenic than Christian in inspiration',[19] though we would have to add that as a solution to the problem of making one figure, by a gesture, dominate that huge wall, it can hardly be faulted. But a much more 'broken' image of Christ comes into Michelangelo's work during his last years, culminating in the literally broken, thin figure of Christ of his final carving, the *Rondanini Pieta*, where the pathos of reality has finally overwhelmed the strong preference for the ideal. Hibbard quotes Panofsky as saying of his late works: 'the dualism between the Christian and

See Plate 18

See Plate 19

---

[18] The influential pioneer of classical art studies, J.J. Winckelmann (1717–1768) came to believe that: 'The only way for us to become great, or inimitable if possible, is to imitate the Greeks' (quoted from biography in *Encyclopaedia Britannica*, 15th ed. 1991, vol. 12, p. 695).

[19] *Michelangelo*, p. 246.

the classical was solved. But it was a solution by way of surrender', [20] meaning that for Michelangelo, the sought-after reconciliation had not been found to be possible; Christian and pagan could not be merged, because one had superseded the other.

The baroque era, of Rubens, of the Carracci, Guercino, Reni, Bernini and Poussin, tried different solutions to the problem of animating the classical inheritance with the Christian spirit, successful in many ways, but in their loquacity and smoothness, always coming up against the stubborn fact of the Cross. However far one is tempted to idealize, the brutality of the Cross, pressing through into art, repeatedly brings up the question of the nature of man and of God, and finally makes a laughing-stock of the gods.

b) Discerning 'the gap'

The idol, then, is well able to exercise persuasive powers of its own, which as we have seen, once there in a culture are very difficult to exorcize. But although they appear to work by being 'information rich', by conveying very powerfully an idea, they actually work by disinformation, conveying a false idea. And as we have seen, the gods are very comfortable and very convincing until put side by side with the real 'image' of God, the man Jesus. Indeed, St Paul's words in Colossians (1:15) about Christ, that 'he is the image of the invisible God' become all the more striking when we think of the images of the gods that were on every street corner in the cities in which those words were read. It is next to the true image of God that the gods made with hands seem empty, and their ideals hollow. Therefore there is, even in the finest and most realistic sculptures, a 'gap' which shows they are not true inhabitants, or rather willing inhabitants of the created world, which might be known in a relational way as art should be known; *but we do not see this until their spell is broken by being brought to a point of comparison with the real world*. Such a gap in their reality is one that we are all too willing to fling ourselves into through our own idealizing tendencies, which presumably is the point at which any demonic influences (as, we must not forget, were welcomed by the ancients) might enter.

c) The gods of the tribes

Now, switching to the diametrically opposite kind of idolatrous image, the masks employed in demon worship in tribal art, we need to see whether any similar principles apply. We should not be too surprised if they do, considering that their appeal in Western art has been felt just at the historical point when the classical gods seemed to have finally expired. We need to picture some of the artefacts in the ethnographic museums that excited Picasso and fellow artists in the 1900s, images that still test

---

[20] Ibid., p. 287.

the border between art and culture, with good reason: weird products of the imagination, inconceivably daring in formal invention; deliberated in concept yet immediate in execution; their human freedom is almost hidden in a terrifying functional directness. They appealed to Picasso as art that worked, that had the power that the flaccid classicism and domesticated naturalism of European art had lost. What was the power?

There is no doubt that when we look at such art, we see it at first through eyes trained in Western idealizing, and it looks more unnatural than it is. When we actually see some of the plants and creatures that inhabit the tropics, the outrageous streaked blue faces of some of the monkeys, the lizards and the patterned snakes, we realize that tribal artists were inhabiting an imaginative world that was of necessity very different from that of the Mediterranean basin. However, it was to the museums rather than to the zoos that Picasso went, and where our attention can still be arrested by a distorted, dislocated figure suddenly glimpsed through the glass of its Victorian mahogany case, reaching past our unguarded cultural defences, to grip us with some devastating insinuation about our condition. Lostness and terror: are they true? We might easily find ourselves fleeing, with Picasso's generation, from the corrupting embrace of the classical ideal, particularly with the carnage of war at hand, and believe so.

Les Demoiselles D'Avignon, that violent demolition of the feminine ideal of Venus, has become an authoritative image of the unredeemable depersonalized entity which, as if the base truth of humanity, stares out mocking from underneath the shattered shell of the goddess. But does the image of God in man, that which cries out for hope and redemption, have to join the fragments of Venus and Apollo in the dustbin? Is depersonalized entity really the human truth, or is it (as St Augustine might have seen it) the demonic core of the idol? There is something about the works of religious technology, the tribal images that so influenced not just Picasso's style but his whole understanding, that distract us from asking this question.

See
Plate
20

It is partly the ambiguity about what they represent. Are they men or demons? A writer on recent finds in prehistoric Chinese art remarks that their 'exaggerated features and enormous eyes . . . to a 20th century observer look downright extra-terrestrial'.[21] This admission helps us not to suppress the possibility that real subhuman creatures are in view, who look inhuman *because they are inhuman*. The chief requirement of this kind of art is for it to represent spirit beings which are by definition disembod - ied, and spiritually sensed (particularly by witch doctors, priests and other specialists), so that the image must give form to entities only 'seen' by the inner eye, though occasionally one reads reports of spirits being seen. The

---

[21] Professor R. W. Bagley, *The Times China Exhibition*, Souvenir Issue, 1996, p. 8.

visual language, therefore, has to be one of metaphor: for example, ways have to be found of expressing the fearsomeness of the demons. One such way is indeed through large, unnatural and blank eyes, which, like hidden spirits, can seem to look out at you without being themselves looked into. But aside from metaphor, there may also be something more 'repre-sentational' about these images, since they are often formed (as 'Hermes' said, and numerous writers have confirmed) to be bodies for the disem-bodied spirits to inhabit. In that sense, they need to be appropriate depictions of the beings that are sensed to exist. But they also need to be 'bodies', (and hence to refer to the only kind of bodies we know, those of human and animal), and so bring the immaterial into nature. This attempt to bridge the physical and spiritual worlds no doubt accounts for some of the ambiguity.

The 'unnatural naturalness' also presumably accounts for the visual power of the primitive image. Where you have a head, a mask or a figure which uses nature, through inversions, distortions and paradoxes to directly assault nature (in order to convey the immaterial), which is yet sufficiently lifelike to participate in nature (to convey the embodying of the immaterial), then you have imaginative presences which appear to be *islands in the whole created order*. I realize this concept is somewhat novel. But the issue remains of the more-than-artistic power of such images, about which Picasso (as recalled by Françoise Gilot), was quite clear; although we will want to go further than him in explanation:

> Men had made those masks and other objects for a sacred purpose, a magic purpose, as a kind of mediation between themselves and the unknown hostile forces which surrounded them . . . I realized that this was what painting was all about. Painting isn't an aesthetic operation; it's a form of magic between this strange, hostile world and us, a way of seizing the power by giving form to our terrors as well as to our desires.[22]

For Picasso, the explanation of the images was as a form of controlling terror by a process of expressing it, bringing it within limits: 'to overcome . . . fear and horror by giving it a form and an image'.[23] A similar process can be experienced when we write down our fears, which immediately has the effect of cutting them down to size. However, this reasoning by no means accounts for the 'magical' power of the images. Picasso describes the power of art in, as it were, capturing the 'unknown forces' and bringing them within the created order, the proper limits of creation; so that we can begin to look on them not as outside but as captive powers; but this does not at all explain why the images actually have the power

---

[22] Quoted by Françoise Gilot in *Life with Picasso*, pp. 248–249.
[23] Ibid., p. 248.

to terrify. Indeed, in the conversation recorded in Gilot's book, which was provoked by the offer to Picasso of a life-size New Guinea fetish by Matisse, Picasso's next remark is, 'Besides . . . that New Guinea thing frightens me. I think it probably frightens Matisse too and that's why he's so eager to get rid of it. He thinks I'll be able to exorcize it better than he can.'[24] The terror is obviously very far from being controlled. What, then, is the process?

We go back to the idea of imaginative presences which appear to be islands in the created order. When thinking about Greek art, we saw there was an attractiveness in the unnaturalness of it, though in this case it was unnatural by being shifted towards the ideal. The primitive images, by contrast, do not allure by being ideal, but dominate by an equal pretension to be extra-natural. This is something more than being unlifelike. If they were merely unlifelike, their unnaturalness would merely be a kind of failure to be natural, what we would call subnatural. Their category (of intention) would not have shifted from the natural, even if the aim had not succeeded. But we are talking of images which, by a strange mental chemistry, we do not compare with nature, because they deliberately convey a life that is beyond nature, through exploiting the inversions and tricks of art to deny nature.

There is therefore created a kind of 'not-nature', which is not exactly another state of being, but more a kind of inversion (instanced by such motifs as 'eyes' represented by protruding cylinders), which depends on our spiritual involvement with its denial of nature to give it life. It exploits, (or introduces us to), the sense of there being a place of non-being, a kind of gap in the fabric of life. Into this 'gap' enters our own willingness to adopt as real the spiritual presuppositions represented in the image, the fear of there being 'holes' in nature, in which real powers can dominate.

The image, then, has a power of taking us away from nature, making something that is markedly less real than nature appear to have greater reality than nature. Any spirit which may be involved (either the subject of the work, or its inspiration), though in itself it is nothing more than a creature, truly a disobedient and hostile creature, but still a part of the created order, is thus able to make its entrance into the world as a 'god'. It is able to pretend to be a power beyond reckoning, on the basis of a kingdom existing in an artistically contrived space, which otherwise does not exist.

Goodness in 'bad' art?

If this seems complicated, that is because any form of evil is complicated; falsehood rides on the back of truth, and what was created good, from art

---

[24] Ibid., p. 249.

to angelic powers, can serve to deceive and promote harm. It is because of this complexity that we are still talking about art, rather than crude religious objects. It is also why it is, to take this thought further, that we cannot simply reject the pagan inheritance generally, and say that the survival of classical thought in Christian theology is bad, and then that the Renaissance revival of the art of paganism is bad, and finally that the stream of demonically inspired (perhaps) tribal art entering the river of Western art in the twentieth century is bad. There may be bad things about it; but that is by no means the whole story.

For even the 'gods' (the fallen angelic beings) that were worshipped in Rome were once created good, and they attracted worship by their association with what was good. The fact that this enabled them to direct worship away from the God who made them does not detract from everything (even abused for bad ends) that was good about them, for there is only one Creator, and as the New Testament author James says, 'every good and perfect gift comes from above' (James 1:17). The fearful beings evoked by tribal art are in a slightly different category, but the human responses to them in worship and creativity are not. Goodness has only one source, even when it is misused and deceptive. Therefore we can uninhibitedly enjoy and employ all that is humanly true in tribal art, its originality, spontaneity and rhythm, in which we can recognize our own natures, and perhaps some of our fears, in very different guise.

However, human craft and the enjoyment of life that goes with it is one thing, and the essence of idolatry as we have tried to outline it is quite another, with a root in deception and a tendency towards death. As a general observation, and thinking of the strong appeal of the informal domestic art of religious societies (e.g. ancient China, Egypt), the less religious and instrumental an art is, the more reliable artistically we find it. And yet there is an appeal and power in the idol image, and this is what we have been trying to define, in relation to all that has been said above about the true qualities of the work of art. It is an appeal we need to be aware of as we assess the flow of art history, particularly into our own times.

Summary

The power of the true, non-idolatrous work of art, the 'small art' that I defined earlier, is that it leads you out into nature, and its meaning, and to truth generally, including the truth of God. It is open, public, accountable, and the artist is servant to the viewer. The viewer comes to 'know' what the artist knows through relational engagement with the world which is shown. Here the artist and viewer are on the same side; the artist is not a priest with a privileged position, controlling access, but a doorman, holding open the door. The power of the idol, by contrast, is that it offers a special experience away from nature, which cannot be publicly checked out in an open way, but has to be entered into. The work, instead of taking its place in nature, within the whole created order, as a vehicle to understand it, operates as a separate entrance (to somewhere else, an alternative idea, an alternative divine government which seems to be preferable) in competition with nature. This can take the form of the free-floating ideal, which at all costs must not be compared with reality; or of its opposite, the presentation of evil powers, as if they alone are in charge.

The experience such works offer is superficially one of knowledge, in that considerable engagement is required. But this private experience does not contend with objective reality; it allows the free access of deceptive notions (and, conceivably, the powers behind them) which have been embodied in the work. If the model of knowledge for the true work of art is relationship, in which there is a kind of equality, the 'knowledge' found through the idol is better described as domination. The feelings of subservience often induced by such works of art, rather than of having been served, are thought of as authentic artistic experience, but to an outside observer look remarkably like worship. Some of these idols actually work.

Chapter Seven

Personal Spiritual Dynamics

The strange appeal of substitutes

And now we come to what is in many ways the most tender part of the book, that which may seem the most intrusive into our own private territory. After all, everyone assumes that, in the area of artistic taste at least, we have a right to ourselves, for our eyes to wander at will, and for our judgements to be our own. Locking the door behind us when we try out works of art has become so habitual, that we would be almost embarrassed for anyone to pry into our soul and see what was going on. When we emerge, we will have made our decisions and our opinions will be our own. And then we suddenly hear it suggested that the respected 'works of art' we have been trying on, are not so much art as idols, and contaminated idols at that. Our private times with art have begun to take on a different public face to the one we had expected. Unless we dismiss the whole idea as either preposterous or repugnant, we might start to question what we have been getting into.

But first of all, it is necessary to clarify just what we have been saying about art and idolatry, *and particularly the demonic*. It is very easy to use words like 'demonic' in a metaphorical sense, or to use 'idol' as a form of innuendo against art we do not like, leaving behind a vague and slightly exciting sense of the spiritual, but in a way that does not directly touch us. That is not the aim here. When we talk about spiritual dynamics, we are not interested in experiences as such. The idol is not defined by what we feel about it, but solely in relationship to the revealed God, whether it is a submitted part of his reality, or whether it represents an alternative source of authority, and a substitute origin of values.

The idol as immovable object

The idol itself, of course, is only an object with no power to submit or to obey. But it represents something which has been willed to exist, and if it cannot act as means of orientation to the real world, because reality as it is (that is, reality which is submitted to God's authority) is not its referent, then it can only open up the notional possibility of an alternative reality. The object is a standing refusal of the world out there, offering more than an 'alternative reading' of nature. It actually proposes an alternative centre. Unlike a person, it cannot be persuaded, or converted. It either does, or does not agree to belong to the world we have. You have to either agree with it (make it a centre), or ignore it, but you cannot dispute with it. This is why, when demon-worshippers are converted to Christ, their first act is to burn their idol-images. That is a part of their lives for which there is no future. Friends and relatives can be converted to the truth, but the idol-image has had its mind made up for it permanently, and has no viability, except possibly as a relic in a museum.

Here we are again, moving without comment between the art gallery and the mission field. Can you be saying that works of art might be idols in any literal sense? We had just got used to the idea of taking items from the museums of ethnology and putting them into the art gallery with the title 'works of art'; and now you seem to be wanting to empty the art galleries, and put the contents back into the ethnology museums, under the heading 'superstitious idols'.

And what's all this about demons? I thought that, at the very least, they needed passports to come into this country, if they exist at all. In any case, art galleries and museums are surely safe.

Well, perhaps we do have difficulties with these ideas, seen from our level, especially given our presupposition of the free, unhindered aesthetic experience. But if God is as important as 'God' actually means, and if he is infallibly executing a plan for every shape, system and spirit on earth, and the rest of the cosmos, to be eventually brought into willing harmony under the authority of one person, Jesus Christ (Ephesians 1:10) – to the effect that there will be nothing left discordant with love, truth and justice as Christ embodies them – then that raises the issue of the general acceptability of this plan, especially to those of us who have vested interests in the present arrangements.

Even putting it mildly, it is entirely possible, given our human freedom, that there are those for whom the ultimacy of Christ as the supreme truth does not appeal, and that consciously or unconsciously they produce works of art which bend the vision of reality to deny him, even if such denial acts only to self-deceptively postpone the inevitable. And it is possible that through such images, the viewer, in the course of understanding them, might be drawn into internal compromises in the way that he or she relates to God. If Jesus is Lord, there is still territory to be played over in the human spirit as to whether that truth is admitted, allowed, or refused.

Art-world values and spiritual fact

Inside the art gallery, we can still sense the battle for values in the art of the past: which system of rule shall seem most attractive, or impressive, and most likely to have the last word. There are the monarchs, and their glory; there is nature, in its glory; there are the myths, Venus and Mars, unredeemable human constants, in their glory; and there is death, the great rival to these, claiming final supremacy. But the battle in our soul for values is different from the issue of fact, that is, which system actually will have the last word, and that has to be settled outside the art gallery. The Christian account is that it has been. This may leave traces in the art inside the gallery (Christian religious art). But it is not the 'values' in the art gallery, those things which art convinces us of, which give substance to the claim.

See
Plate
22   Perhaps I might illustrate this from personal experience. My favourite picture as a child was the great Holbein, *The Ambassadors*. Two men in the prime of life, one dressed in the sobriety of brown fur-lined damask, the other in a profusion of slashed and padded velvet and silk, stand beside a table stacked with instruments of music and learning. To a child, the 'meaning' of the picture resided clearly in the artist's enjoyment of the things, of surfaces, and stuffs, which unmistakably were also the accessories of power. Wealth, learning, and beauty, communicated with uninhibited delight in fabric and finish, had a potent savour, which I carried with me when away from the painting. These are, in a sense, the painting's 'values'. But the artist has attempted to balance these, or even check them, with a 'fact'. At the base of the painting, as if suspended in the air, a skull is depicted, in such optical distortion that, not only can one not fail to notice it, but it functions like a line of cancellation: 'No, these things last not!' But a skull, in itself, is almost an inert fact. 'Death' may well heighten, as much as challenge, the charms of the good things of life. So one further fact is introduced, which as a child I did not even notice, until I read about it. Behind a curtain is glimpsed a crucifix. This is a small reminder of a very big alternative values-system. But it is a sign: it does not communicate by artistic power. Like the lighted Exit sign in a theatre, it is in no way part of the play. It is simply an external reference to a fact one might need. And it only 'works', indeed it is only relevant, if that 'fact' actually has buying power in reality. It is the fact, not the picture, which settles whether power, position and possession are ultimates.[25]

A statement is made in one of the gospels which defines, for all time, the substance of the 'fact', that the values that the world presents to us have been, in actuality, relativized. 'All authority in heaven and on earth has been given to me', says the resurrected Jesus to his disciples (Matthew 28:18) in what must be the most totally encompassing credible claim to power ever uttered by human lips, only credible from the manifest victor in a battle, in which the pretensions of every other authority had been

---

[25] This illustration of the relation of facts to values is not being offered as an interpretation of the Holbein, though it should be consistent with it. A fascinating and compatible explanation is given in Derek Wilson's *Hans Holbein, Portrait of an Unknown Man*, pp. 193–201, 211.

exposed and destroyed. Which are the rival authorities now made subject? One could do worse than to list the employers and tasks of artists down the centuries, to describe the 'thrones' (ideologies and systems) which attempt to rule, and spiritual powers which try to work through them. Which is not, of course, to say that those powers always, or even often, have had the upper hand in art. But art is not goodness, exposed and confronting evil, in quite the way that Jesus was. Jesus brought the perfection of his character, his refusal of any compromise with evil, into direct and lonely confrontation not only with death and disease, but with corrupt religious and political power, and in such a way that it thought it had won. And we really need to know which of them has won, whether goodness is ultimately 'worthwhile', whether truth, which sometimes seems so weak, will be vindicated.

Fall of the dictators
Jesus knew it, but the resurrection demonstrated it, that the powers of evil, state powers, religious powers, hypocrisy, cowardice, betrayal, lies and cruelty do not have, even if they seem to have, the final say. The 'powers', those apparent fixed points of the present order, which had seemed so strong, all-conquering in the might of Rome and its gods, and all-pervasive in the cunning of Judea and its priests, had been shown to be weak. So weak, in fact, considering what they had tried to do to Jesus and had failed to do (to stamp out his existence and memory), that he had 'made a public example' of them, as St Paul reflected, in the aftermath of that contest (Colossians 2:15). Like fallen dictators, whose statues have been toppled, their offices and files opened and emptied, and their papers strewn in the palace yard, the names of the powers were suddenly without force or fear. To everyone's surprise, good had the mastery. And the powers, which might have forced us to say good things about them, could be seen for the rogues they are.

But this 'fact' has not yet been seen in its completion. Notice has been served on the false powers,[26] but eviction has not taken place. Until the day of completion, we are in the time of choices, in which art is caught up, aligning either with what will remain, or what will go. Art can have a role in unmasking false ultimates, even though alone it does not establish the truth, which as we have said, has to exist in fact. Sometimes it even unmasks itself. Few works of art are as silly as the gilded statue of Lenin that was proposed for the apex of a Moscow skyscraper. Those now discarded monuments to dictators, which seriously try to divinize a man, are monuments to the bathos of the aim. There is something about art itself, as we have seen, that is resistant to untruth, and whose quality and dignity is emptied out by too gross an alliance with propaganda. But the

---

[26] For very helpful discussion of 'the powers' in the New Testament, see the works by N.T. Wright listed in the Bibliography.

fact that some of the most transparently hollow idolatry has failed to convince artists does not indicate that all idolatry has, or that there is not still in art a battleground for the allegiance of the human soul.

Here we are not trying to say that this or that work of art 'is an idol', or to go through the canon of great art making a checklist of those that fail to meet some test. We are for art, and especially for the fact that even in some of the most probably demon-inspired art we find qualities of life, truth and freedom. What we are saying is that if, in this time of choices, the human heart is still looking for let-outs from the gospel of Christ, that there is a collusion possible of works of art with that. And such works will make it seem as if nothing of what we have just described has happened. Death and destruction, evil and nature are still in charge; the material world is ultimate; pleasure is the only god. We need not have any resentment towards the works which purvey such ideas. They are still art; but they may not be of any use. In a sense they are like holograms; we can look at them from one side, and see something reflected of the Creator's glory; but shifting a little to see into their idea system, we find mere values, powerfully held, but ultimately obsolete.

Art as secular religion

All that we have said implies that our secular world is no less engaged with religious meaning, and crossed with buried power lines of religious activity, than the world of the first century, in which 'gods' had names and statues. It implies too that works of art may have as significant a place in the force fields of spiritual power as did images for Rome, and as do the fetishes of the tribal world. If all this still seems to take art too seriously, we might ask ourselves what is the source of the image-hunger which is such a prevalent feature of today's world.

There is one obvious source, which is in a way quite healthy: the hunger for meaning. Our scientific world has so drained out meaning, and our need for it is so great, that we do not just go to art, but even allow unscrupulous advertisers to put it back. If they want to package 'family' into frozen food, we will let them, for it is the only place we will get it; if they want to offer us the peace of a cruise in a bottle of booze, we will let them, for that harmony is not, apparently, found anywhere else. Who goes into a church for it? Who believes that heaven on earth is possible, except in an alcoholic haze? There is also a hunger for the ordinary meanings that things should have, which continues to rejuvenate the art of earlier times. The *Times* journalist Simon Jenkins has a good eye for this, and in a couple of pieces piqued the sophistries of catalogue writers by pointing out that the underlying theme of Vermeer's work was home and family, and of Cézanne's was the countryside, and its bounty. I am not sure the appeal of Cézanne is that simple: perception with him is like a battle fought, and that, as well as his subjects, is something we moderns relate to. But we can conclude that it is partly their recognition of the intrinsic meanings in those things, that have made those painters popular. We have got to know that 'things' are more than appearances, and have substance, and value, and purpose, and pleasure.

But there is another hunger for images, that not only of those who have found, but also the hunger of the lost. Those drawn to art, to judge from gallery-goers (sometimes one cannot help noticing the viewers, as well as the pictures), can look the least satisfied of people; there is something about them (to my eye) which often seems to be looking, but not finding. They are looking, apparently, for their 'proper image', that which answers their need to find themselves; or at least looking for a compass to orient them in the world. The search goes on, from exhibition to exhibition. The writer Germaine Greer, quoted on an exhibition poster for *Late Braque*, says she would like to 'park her bed' at that show: she has found her home. Others will move on from Braque's dislocated studios disappointed, and try to find their home elsewhere. This is a search for the world, but it is also a search for me: 'what am I, who am I?' It is a private, person-to-artist, soul-to-soul quest for recognition of that in us which we think might be there. Tell me this is not a religious search.[27]

The difficulty with the term 'religious search', however, is that it sounds so innocent, particularly if we are the ones doing the searching. But sex, drugs, alcohol and greed and other captivities may also have something about them of the religious search, as we try to press mere matter to elicit the meaning we crave. A religious search may be proceeding in us, but we may be degraded by it nonetheless.

We might also wonder what kind of search this is. Any search should, after a while, reveal whether the thing being sought has actually been found. There is no sense in continuing a religious search in the wrong direction. But we also know that common sense is seldom the first priority in matters religious; many people seem to be unable to do other than knowingly to destroy their minds and bodies in their 'religion' until set free from something which holds them.

It is as if the presupposition of the search is wrong. It is not that there is a refusal of the costs of the search: many costly quests have been undertaken, not least by artists pursuing their thoughts to ultimate destinations, which has cost them everything in a life, health, family, friends; but it has been an acceptance of the wrong cost. Searching leaves us in control. The greater cost is the encounter *by* truth, allowing ourselves to be seen for what we are.

---

[27] See Jacques Barzun, 'The Rise of Art as Religion', in his Mellon Lectures, *The Use and Abuse of Art*, 1974; in an *Encyclopaedia Britannica* article the same author describes 'the cult of art' as 'at the present time the main outlet for spirituality among Western intellectuals' (15th ed., vol. 18, p. 702).

All this means that the self-doctoring of religion is not necessarily either clean or healthy. We are not necessarily the best servants for our bodies, minds or spirits; we are too likely to be pursuing our own compromises. Therefore leaping into the void of art (if that is the manifestation of our religious quest) may appear to be a most intelligent and cultured thing to do, but it may also be most stupid. Religion, if not good, is harm. The worlds of art, the paths inside the canvases, may lock people into ways of thinking in which they think they are free, but from which they need to escape. They think they have found, but they have been taken. I might sound as if I talk from personal experience. I do.

★ ★ ★

But surely there is a difference between the direct religion of the ancient and modern worlds, and the freedom of the art gallery? I am sure there is, but I am not sure that we should expect the demonic powers to recognize it. Anything which orients the mind and spirit is likely to be fair game for their attentions. *There you go, talking about demons again. What exactly are you trying to imply? Are you trying to scare us?*

First of all, I am trying to inject a little spiritual reality into all the talk of religion. Religion is not a game we play on our own. There are other players as well. They do not necessarily disclose who or what they are, because that is part of the game. But, as has been almost universally found in every religion, 'there is something there'. That something, or those somethings, have an interest in gaining our interest, and in drawing us deeper into spirit-to-spirit contact with them. Some people like to blindly believe that the 'something there' is just one thing, and that everything with which they may come into contact behind the curtain of visibility is 'God'. But experience, terrifying experience, of the things people do at the suggestion of those 'somethings', hardly bears this out. These days, plenty of people do not need to read St Augustine to know what we are talking about. They have had direct contact with the spirit world through seances, and through fringe, or deeper, occult activities. Some people have had such frightening experiences that they have known straightaway that they must leave such things alone.

None of this appears, at first sight, to have much bearing on art. The interests of the 'something there' are obviously best served by direct contact, direct control of their human channels, and direct worship, in which the submission of the human soul is most complete. There is indeed a difference between the idol temple and the temple of art, for the former has a focus and intention, which the latter does not. It is a free place. The image in the idol temple has one way of appropriate reverence: the same image in the art museum can be seen in many ways. But it does not follow that demons lose all interest in the human soul except where they are directly worshipped. There is always the first touch, the initial contact. The modern art museum is, shall we say, propitious for them, for it is a place in which, under the respectable covering of culture, certainties are apt to be dissolved, foundations weakened, and questions opened, all at the sub-critical level of how we perceive things to be. This is a place where confusion can be engendered: the characteristic modern condition of being unable to see distinctions, because widely disparate things have been fused together. The mind of someone leaving an art gallery can be very different to how it was when they went in. Who can say that the internal commerce of the mind in such places is of no concern to demonic powers?

Worst case scenario (moments with Mondrian)
We want to try to be as specific as possible. The problem with writing about demons, however, is that in many ways they are quite comic. It is not just that, in the traditions of church art, in Romanesque carvings and gothic gargoyles, they often have such entertainingly grotesque faces. It is rather that there is something inherently comic about a human being who is being led about by something as wretched as a demon, rather like those unfortunates who are completely under the domination of an ill-tempered and all-demanding pet. When the human is so gullible, you can almost forgive the animal for getting away with it! In the same way, demons may not be very important in the actual balance of spiritual forces. It is the wandering human will which is the great power. But as with some pets, so with demons: they will exploit weaknesses, and given an inch will certainly take a mile. So it is not impossible for them to enter at the slightest beckoning, and to stay, take over and thoroughly disorganize your home.

So how would this happen with art? The following did not happen to me, but perhaps could have done. I am in London's Tate Gallery, looking at a Mondrian. The picture's label informs me that Mondrian's Neo-plasticism, derived from theosophy, embodies the belief that there is a 'purely spiritual part of the human mind'. This sounds good. I am sick of empty materialism. Someone who believes that there is a spiritual side of us must be on my side. Theosophy sounds good, too, with such a respected artist backing it. At least, it sounds as if it might be able to get me onto a spiritual level without too many moral catches. And from what I have heard, it sounds tolerant, so it must be ethically OK. So here I am, ready for a spiritual experience. At first I am disconcerted. What could be spiritual about those grids of lines? I thought 'spiritual' things were fluid and organic. But as I enter in to the imaginary space, I find that, although it is not organic, there is a fluency. Something is going on through the squares and behind the squares. The grids give me something to hold onto, but they are not themselves the space. Inside and behind the grids is a shallow space which seems to hover, just outside and beyond this reality. At one corner, a yellow square gives a puff of misty gold, inviting me beyond. Reality, says this experience, is away from here. This empty material thing-world is not the real thing at all, not leaves and blood and mud and all that stuff. Real reality is for the 'purely spiritual part of the human mind' to reside in, leaving the tiresome body behind. 'Come hither, friend, this is the place of purity and peace. Come and be one in your mind with this emptied-out spiritual place. Find rest, find freedom in this space where no cares are; and come beyond, to the glowing light, which is only just beyond: trust it, and enter in'.

'*No thank, you, Mr Mondrian.* I do respect you immensely for what you have done; I would not have known such an experience was possible through paint, and least of all, through abstract paint, but thank you, no. Having considered all that you have to offer, I have decided to stay with reality as I know it. It is not that I am not intrigued by the idea of spirit divorced from body: I can see its attractions. It certainly lets me off the hook of my troubles down here. In many ways I should like to fly off to a place where there is only me and a glorified nothingness, especially if you promise that it is the real thing, and that everything else that bothers will disappear, as in a dream. But it is not what I really want or need. What interests me is the redemption, not the abnegation, of this disor - dered world. For myself what I need is something that speaks of the remaking, not the disappearance, of my bodily condition. And the Spirit that I believe in does not just leave the world behind, like an anxious babysitter who cannot cope, but joins in to sort the mess out. In fact this Spirit does not despise the particularity of the physical world, as if it was only the wearying substitute for the real thing. He brooded over it in the first place, to bring it into being (Genesis 1:2). He does not abstract himself from it. He touches it.'

But suppose I had no such foundations in Genesis, etc. and could not so easily dialogue with Mondrian. Suppose the vision tempted me. Perhaps I might have been looking for a spiritual exit. Perhaps I would be willing to toy with the idea of there being a more 'real', though impersonal world. Mondrian was, after all, painting what he really believed was the case. I might then start to entertain the thought that he was right. Combining that thought with the desire that he should be right, I could mentally enter into such a world – which does no harm, because it does not exist – but at that point of thought it is possible that some *spiritual entity* might station itself, to help provide some such experience; and what is more important, to close the door behind it. The thought that I have desired will have been reinforced by such a spirit, amplified to become stronger than what my senses tell me. From then on, there will be something duller about my vision of this present reality. It will be there, but it will not be as much there. The dulling of the senses is one thing that demonized, or formerly demonized people will testify to.

This all sounds bad, and it is bad, because it represents a robbery of the very physical world which God created to testify to himself. It represents a theft of hope, of everything which has been created good in this life and which of itself cries out for resolution and redemption. It represents the obliteration by a blank grid, by the ideality of impersonal nothingness, of the face of a personal creator, who cares to lift up and cradle each of his children. Such an experience, multiplied across the great range of art which implicitly denies the Creator, the Son, and the Spirit, also provides something of an explanation of the terrible deadness towards God, the head-shaking deafness to the majesty of the divine sound, which is so often found among supposedly 'spiritually minded' artistic people. It also helps explain the strange opacity of thinking in the art press, where even high intelligence seems to get overwhelmed in the confused current.

Unexpected results of demonization

None of this, incidentally, is easy to write about. This is not only because we are dealing with an invisible realm, which leaves its footprint in the culture but is not itself our object of study. Indeed it is invisible presumably for the good reason that we do not need to know very much about it. Any false ideas in the art press or anywhere else still have to be dealt with according to the rules of rational argument, rather than with swords, not to mention bonfires. But we do need to be especially aware of the need for the sharpness of truth, because so much of what passes for argument happens first at a pre-rational level. As everyone knows, strong ideological pulls, which may be spiritually coloured, guide thought, and it is all too easy for the mind to be, as it were, pulled out of shape.

But an equal difficulty is not just the invisibility of those beings who are all too willing to lend their ideas to our thought processes, but the fact that what they do is so counter-intuitive. It might be easy to spot their work if they always came up with 'bad' statements. Here is one such. The art critic Suzi Gablik quotes a provocative example from Jean-Francois Lyotard, the French deconstructionist. At one level what he says is an understandable, if ironically exaggerated, response to cultural exhaustion. But at another level, it is an unmasked advocacy of wrong.

> 'Here is a course of action', he writes, responding to a culture whose ideals he sees as a hollow mask, 'harden, worsen, accelerate decadence . . . adopt the perspective of active nihilism . . . Become more and more incredulous. Push decadence further still and accept, for instance, to destroy the belief in truth under all its forms.' [28]

All right: let's try it. 'Harden' means to lose all compassion, to believe no one's story, to live only for oneself. Here is an end of society. 'Accelerate decadence'? Easily done; we promote more and more pornography, sado-masochism, adultery, fornication, divorce, child abuse, incest. One

---

[28] Gablik, *The Reenchantment of Art*, p. 16.

wonders what further percentage of society needs to be involved in this to achieve utter decadence; which would mean the final destruction of the family and therefore of any prospect of emotional and social health. Then we destroy trust, by becoming 'incredulous'. We refuse to trust anyone, which would mean the abolition of business and trade; and we destroy the idea of truth, which would eliminate justice and education.

The unfortunate fact is that similar such experiments have already been tried, very successfully, at various moments in places like China, Russia, Cambodia, and very often such evils have had an intellectual source. Whole societies have been for a short time in the grip of ideas which instantly lay waste the social fabric, of trust, civility, service, respect, the grounding of the arts, which it has taken centuries to achieve. (I have already mentioned the account of the Chinese Cultural Revolution in *Wild Swans*, which may stand for all such events.)

The odd thing is, that we can feel the appeal of Lyotard's rhetoric, as if it is an answer to the perceived hollowness of the modern age. Every revolutionary seems to think the cure for a pain in the foot is a blow on the head. The very fact that we can almost be convinced by such lurid ideas, which if actually carried out would certainly put to an end all such leisurely philosophy as Lyotard's, shows that such thoughts could have an inhuman source. They warp their way around our own rationality.

But if we listen to what the New Testament has to say about demon-inspired ideas, something far more ominous emerges. There is something almost satisfying about identifying the extremes of evil we have just discussed. But demonic ideas in the New Testament are much more like the pollution that we daily breathe. They are not, as we would expect, messages arising in seances, or among occult activists. They are part of the normal discussion among people about the best way to live; but some of those popular notions happen to have an outside source.

The examples that St Paul gives of 'doctrines of demons' and the work of 'deceiving spirits' are ideas of breathtaking respectability. The current talk was of abstinence from marriage and from certain foods. Very moral, no doubt, and very self-denying such ideas must have seemed. It took a Paul, guided by the Holy Spirit, to see that the root of such ideas was a refusal of the sumptuous world God had created, and hence of the Creator himself; and to see that this twisting away from grateful relationship with God had inspired not outright apostasy, but acts of apparent morality and self-denial, which were of no actual benefit to anyone.

> Now the Spirit expressly says that in later times some will depart from the faith by giving heed to deceitful spirits and doctrines of demons, through the pretensions of liars whose consciences are seared, who forbid marriage and enjoin abstinence from foods which God created to be received with thanksgiving by those who believe and know the truth. For everything created by God is good . . . (1 Timothy 4:1–4)

We are back, to some extent, in the world of Mondrian: experiencing a 'buzz' from denying matter, when what in fact we are doing is denying God.

Art and morality

Being naturally religious creatures, and delighting in our own moral efforts, it is very difficult for us to imagine how great an investment the demonic powers might have in religion and morality. The classical religions were for the most part very moral, at least in some of their ideas, though with large gaps in performance, and 'the world religions' of today are also much concerned with morality; indeed, there is little else for them to do. I know I exaggerate. But sometimes in the West we have been astonished to find the recognition of right and wrong in the 'other religions', as if that raised them to a high ethical plane. But every society knows that morality is needed if it is going to survive. However none of this vast exercise in setting boundaries and laying down the law has done anything for the salvation of the immoral person.

Art is also able to be employed in moral exercises. Some of them may be 'spirit'-affirming and life-denying, some of them may emphasize effort, or society, or community, or many good things to try to put the world right. But if that is all they do, they are departing in no wise from the agenda of the powers that crucified Jesus. It is not that Jesus is not for all those good things. One day he will have them all knocked into shape: morality, community, ecology, the lot. But there is something important that is being left out. The cart is coming before the horse, indeed that the cart needs a horse is not remembered at all. The agenda of the powers is to have us forget that, before we can fix this world, someone from the outside has to come into it, and become part of it, and fix it from within – and that this has actually happened.

The centre of this event is what is known as 'the blood of Christ', real human blood, offered in flesh, as flesh, by God, for God, through which alone the abiding curse on life and the world is lifted. It is a terrible event needing to be kept secret, as far as the powers are concerned, for by that blood they have no more right to any kind of dominion over the human creatures, any that avail themselves of it. This is nothing to do with morality. Morality may help them keep the secret. Good art and good culture may also hide the secret. But what does not hide the secret so well is real flesh-and-blood life.

Christ between two thieves; this is the beauty of God, but it is hardly most people's ideal. It is not nearly spiritual enough. But that image is the heart of the truth about our world and God, which a picture of 'Christ' suspended in a blank or golden empyrean can never be. By extension, anything of flesh and blood, not analytic science, but the world as it abuts on experience, has the capacity to lead to theological reality. The stuff of the world does get us from here to there. Creation and the need for redemption are all there, and the truth that redemption has to have happened 'down here'. The test for discerning evil spirits given by St John is whether they refuse to acknowledge that 'Jesus Christ has come in the flesh' (1 John 4:2). Which must be why there is such demonic hostility to the things which sustain life, to marriage and to food, and perhaps why there has been such a battle in art, in our very religious century, for the maintenance of the object and the visible world.

Images: from prohibition to provisionality

The art gallery, then, is a place where much more may be at stake than even the most conceptual or intellectualized account of art usually allows. We are, at the very least, talking about an aesthetic pill with cognitive side-effects! But some of these side-effects may have consequences for real being (spiritual receptiveness to truth), depending on the resistance, or openness, of the viewer. If this seems complicated, it merely indicates the risks and responsibilities that we have been allowed in living with images. It also helps explain the comprehensiveness of the Second Commandment, in which all kinds of 'likenesses' were comprehensively forbidden the people of God (Exodus 20:4). Indeed for the amount of trouble images can cause, it may seem sensible to ask, in the spirit of Exodus, whether they are worth the risk. Living without them would seem much simpler!

The Second Commandment: needed or superseded?

It is helpful to see the dangers of imagery in respect of the parallel concern that some Islamic communities have with that equal heart-turner, female beauty. Beauty and sexual attraction are facts of life; either, within social restraints, a powerful social cement, or else, in the present habits of the West, one of the most powerful social solvents. One sympathizes with those to whom those 'present habits' must seem like an attempt to electrically wire a house without any form of insulation! It must seem hardly surprising if, often enough, the house burns down. The very practical Islamic 'solution' to this 'problem' is to hide the female form altogether from public view, just as also they ban alcohol and images. But surely there is also a cost in this to the general health of society. What looks to outsiders like a censorship of creation does make one wonder whether such risk-free living was intended. There must be a better way of living with the risks.

The fact that such 'risks' as beauty are necessary for the full enjoyment of the Creator's world indicates that there must be more to salvation than shutting parts of the world down. In fact the very power of beauty as a fact of creation teaches us to look away from our divided responses to it, and towards the saving presence of God. That openness to God under the eye of temptation is a luxury we can afford, once we believe in Salvation as a fact of history. Likewise, the historical dimension of salvation helps us also to see images as a potentially manageable fact of creation. In its time, the prohibition of the Second Commandment was absolute, but in 'the fullness of time' when Jesus came, it came to seem more like a promise of the true image that had now come. The gospel did not abolish, but superseded it. The Old Testament ban on image-making is understandable as an absolute safeguard for a people whose vision of the ultimacy of the invisible, Creator God was always liable to lose focus in favour of the immediate and easily imaged. But once the true image of God was revealed in the Son, Jesus Christ, then images themselves came to lose much of their force. When the original had come, the street-value of imitations began to decline.

As the church came to recognize early, though not without immense struggle, the incarnation of God in Jesus Christ put images in a new category. They could no longer compete as representations of God. Their sphere of operation was restored to its proper level, as objects within creation. They could function as practical signs for that which God had revealed of himself (but without attempting to add any new knowledge), in the spiritual and physical dimension. Or they could fulfil that role of creative human extension which, to some extent, the covenant with Moses had restricted (although, as if to compensate, the great works of art which were the tabernacle and Temple were given particular attention in the Bible). Images were liberated to become adjuncts of Creation rather than substitutes for God.

The teaching of Christ, while in some ways more demanding even than the Law, was also instrumental in liberating the image. By putting his finger on the evil in us, rather than on that which assails us, he opened up the principle of self-control, making it feasible to handle such radio - active substances as sex and images, turning them into power stations, rather than bombs. He was probably speaking more about sexual lust than idolatry when he said 'If your eye offend you, pluck it out' (Mark 9:47), but the same emphasis would apply in both cases: take responsibility for what is in you, rather than try to destroy what is before you. St Paul, who confronted idolatrous images more frequently than was ever necessary even in Roman-ruled Israel, did not preach destruction on them. He freely pointed out how inadequate they were:

Being then God's offspring, we ought not to think that the Deity is like gold, silver, or stone, a representation by the art and imagination of man. The times of ignorance God overlooked. (Acts 17:16,29–30)

His 'attack' on images was only to preach something superior. It is remarkable that when his preaching provoked a riot in pagan Ephesus, it was agreed on all sides that though Paul's teaching was likely to result in the eventual decline and overthrow of Diana, the city's goddess, he himself had not been 'sacrilegious' or a 'blasphemer' against her (Acts 19:37). He had no need to insult her, because he was quite free of any temptation to be impressed by her.

There are only two of the Ten Commandments which are not precisely reaffirmed in the New Testament, the Sabbath law, and the law against image-making, and it is striking that both have been fulfilled in Christ. Christ is the 'Lord of the Sabbath', the one in whom the true 'Sabbath rest for the people of God' takes place, and he is also the true 'image' of God. In neither case does it mean that the Commandments are cavalierly abandoned, as of no further interest. It means instead that under the New Covenant, the Sabbath is held lightly, as pointing to something greater, and similarly, when we look at images we do so in the knowledge that God has the right to call us away from them at any time, that we may concentrate on his full disclosure in his Son. So instead of banning images, God has under the New Covenant utterly relativized them, exposing their provisional nature. With the true Image of God in place, images arrive at a relaxed liberation. Delivered from the stress of inventing ultimates, they take their place as a tool of expression, and as a free and pleasurable extension of humanity.

Relaxing with art

Relaxed liberation: an intriguing thought; there is indeed something that has happened to release the flood-tide of European art. It is strange to think it could have been an event as 'inartistic', in human terms, as the Cross of Christ. The conclusion then, is that Christ is better for art, in setting it free to be itself, and he is also better with art, to free us from art's religious attractions to enjoy it.

Of course, it would be happy for us if that had also been the verdict of history. The defeat of 'the gods' in the late Roman empire must have seemed so final, as temples and statues were hacked to pieces, to be discovered by artists and archaeologists hundreds of years later. But the human project was not finished, it merely went underground (literally underground, given the impact of the art that was rediscovered) for a while. Which is not to say that pagan art could not be triumphantly re-employed under the government of Christ. But it does indicate that the battle of the idols was far from over.

The New Testament writers, incidentally, never did suppose that the danger of idolatry would go with the exit of the idols. The human heart, it seems, no sooner throws out one kind of false saviour before it fixes on another. In a phrase which applies to many of us would-be art owners, talent promoters, and thing-worshippers, St Paul almost off-handedly refers to 'covetousness, which is idolatry' (Colossians 3:5, also Ephesians

5:5). Those of us who have felt driven by irrational lusts for ownership will know what he means. It is as if the whole Old Testament battle with the gods of the nations for the heart of Israel, and the challenge of the Church to the temples of Greece and Rome, has been compacted into one phrase, which exposes the deceptiveness and secrecy of the human heart. If anything as vast as false worship could be hidden in the normal, furtive lust for possessions, then it is not surprising that art, which appeals to us not just sensually but at the level of ideas, can spiritually be a minefield. In the next part, we will look at how the battle of the idols has continued into our own time.

Plate 1 Jacob Ruisdael (1628/9-82)
Extensive landscape with a Ruined Castle and a Village Church, c1665-70 National
Gallery, London
*Ruisdael, a painter who does not so much make spiritual symbols from the landscape, as find
them, speaking from a language already there.* See p. 6.

Plate 2 Paul Nash (1889-1946)
The Menin Road, 1919 Imperial War Museum, London, by permission
*'It is unspeakable, godless, hopeless', wrote the painter with a mission to tell the truth about the
war; but his brush could not refuse - though his mind recoiled from it - the 'blasphemous' offering
of beauty.* See p. 7.

Plate 3 Rembrandt van Rijn (1606–69)
Self Portrait, c 1665 Kenwood House, Hampstead, London, photo English Heritage Photographic Library

The self-portrait in which you can see yourself - and humanity's condition: greatness almost swallowed up by self-harm; and self-reproach almost yielded to forgiveness. See p. 7.

Plate 4 Diego Velasquez (1599–1660)
Pope Innocent X, 1650 Galleria Doria Pamphili, Rome, photo Bridgeman Art Library

The intimate of Spanish royalty and his sitter are agreed: the pope also is a man. A man used to dominating, but also dominated; not so much by the fierce eye of the artist, as by the shared fear of God. See p.8.

Plate 5 John Constable (1776–1837) Lane near East Bergholt with a Man Resting (oil on board, 21.6 cm x 32.7 cm) dated Oct 13, 1809 English Private Collection, by kind permission of owner, photo courtesy Agnew's

Constable's relaxed poise in the landscape signifies not a detached, but an attached objectivity, a spiritual openness to marvel in the ordinary: 'The landscape painter must walk in the fields with a humble mind. No arrogant man was ever permitted to see nature in all her beauty . . . I would say most emphatically to the student, "remember now thy Creator in the days of thy youth" ' (Discourses, p. 71). See p. 21.

Plate 6 Titian (Tiziano Vecellio) (c1487/90–1576) The Death of Actaeon, c1565 National Gallery, London

The collapse of fortune under the arrow of fate: the pagan experience rendered here with Christian empathy. A storm in paint serves subject and feeling; large gestures still controlled by form. See p. 42.

Plate 7 J.M.W. Turner (1775–1851)
Fort Vimieux, exh RA 1831 English Private Collection, by kind permission of owner,
photo courtesy Agnew's
*'The sun is god', Turner is supposed to have said. Does he observe the sun differently from
Rubens? To my eye, his sun looms like an enemy, rather than singing like a friend, closing in on
the stricken ship as if nearer than the far shore; bewitching matter into mist. Nonetheless, a
wonderful rendering of nature.* See p. 57.

Plate 8 Sir Peter Paul Rubens (1577–1640)
Landscape, Chateau de Steen, c1635–7 National Gallery, London
*Rubens' sun, a friend of the day, and perhaps a begetter of life, but not a god. How proportionate
Rubens' treatment of nature is; everything alive, fulfilling its part in the economy of well-being;
nothing over-dominates; the sun one singer in the chorus of creation.* See p. 58.

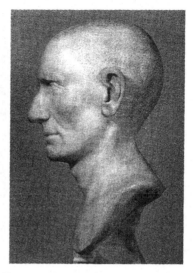

Plate 9 Statue of Apollo 2nd century AD
Roman copy, from Temple of Apollo at Cyrene, of Hellenistic original of 200–150 BC British Museum, London, photo copyright Trustees of BM. See pp. 58, 85.

Plate 10 Roman portrait bust, c30–10 BC
British Museum, London, photo copyright Trustees of BM. See p. 58.

Plate 11 Roman portraits: funerary relief of a priest and his wife, c30–10 BC
British Museum, London, photo copyright Trustees of BM

If the 'gods' of Rome were not so disturbingly close, as with Apollo here, to some pop idol images of today, we would perhaps question why a society with such an obvious grasp of the real, should be so fixated on the ideal. See p. 58.

Plate 12 Albrecht Dürer (1471-1528)
St Jerome, c.1495-6 National Gallery, London

No artist has been more focussed on the material creation than this, from cloud to lovingly observed birch-stump; but where, with this intensity of eyesight, does he take us? Through the saint's 'inward gaze', to feast on the God who made it all. The contingent creation perfectly understood: complete, free, yet reflecting God. See pp. 60 and 80.

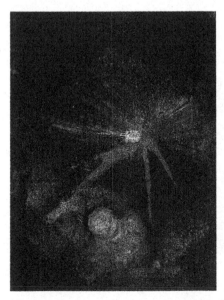

Plate 13 Dürer
St Jerome, back of picture, a Heavenly Body (possibly a falling star from Revelation) National Gallery, London

The artist also free: artists, it is sometimes supposed, 'must' obey the styles of their time; but the 'modern' paint-spattering on the reverse of the St Jerome, shows that the 'medieval detail' of the face was also part of the painter's freedom. See p. 60.

Plate 14 Jan van Eyck (d1441)
The Arnolfini Marriage, 1434
National Gallery, London

'Jan van Eyck was here' states an inscription in Latin, a fact which hardly needs stating, when we are so much in debt to the cool, penetrating, and active observation of the artist; but it stands to exemplify the personal in objectivity, the hidden, but vital presence of a witness. See p. 68.

Plate 15 Domenico Ghirlandaio (1449-94)
An Old Man and a Boy, Louvre, Paris,
photo Bridgeman Art Library

The man enveloped by the love he gives; the painter has observed, not just his disfigurement, but a truth of being, in which the desire to patronize him disappears; for though his 'outer man' is wasting away, his 'inner man' has been renewed, irradiating his face with a quiet beauty, echoed in the landscape. See p. 79.

**Plate 16 Titian (Tiziano Vecellio)
(c1487/90–1576)**
Portrait of Emperor Charles V, 1548 Munich
Alte Pinakotek, photo Giraudon/Bridgeman
Art Library

*By title, Charles was in the succession of the Roman emperors, but has himself portrayed very
differently. Here is no man-god, one who claims the height and glory for himself; he sits more
humbly, with the space of God above him, and the space of creation around him.* See p. 79.

**Plate 17 Sir Anthony van Dyck (1599–
1641)**
Lord John Stuart and his brother Lord
Bernard Stuart, c1638 National Gallery,
London

*. . . but human glory does 'work': the frank enjoyment of privilege, and its accessories, is evident
in these careless aristocrats, and in the artist's display of them as they would wish to be; but a
hint, in his too-honest portraiture, of a heedless pride, and in that nervous drapery, of the
transience of life, was too sadly fulfilled; both brothers were to die in the Civil War.* See p. 83.

Plate 18 Michelangelo Buonarroti (1475-1564)
The Last Judgement, 1536-41, detail of Christ Sistine Chapel, Vatican, Rome, photo Scala Florence

The figure of Christ 'has always been recognised as more Hellenic than Christian in inspiration' (Hibberd): power and authority represented by looks and muscle; by which the artist aims to render a more commanding presence than has yet been seen on earth (see his presumed source, Matthew 24:29-31). See p. 85.

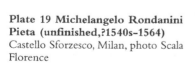

Plate 19 Michelangelo Rondanini Pieta (unfinished,?1540s-1564)
Castello Sforzesco, Milan, photo Scala Florence

Christ in his humiliation, not his glory, and the focus no longer on outer strength, but on the inward beauty of his spent body. See p. 85.

**Plate 20 Pablo Picasso
(1881–1973)**
Les Demoiselles D'Avignon,
1907 Museum of Modern
Art, New York, copyright
Succession Picasso/DACS
1998

*Faces say too much, they engage with the potential for relationship; which is not what Picasso
was after in his painting, which is more concerned with the transformation, mainly by denying
clear space to the observer, of vulnerability into power; so it is not surprising that the faces were
the artist's greatest problem area, only 'solved' by turning two of them into masks.* See p. 87

Plate 21 Picasso
Portrait of Daniel-Henry
Kahnweiler, 1910 (oil on canvas,
100.6cm x 72.8cm) Art Institute of
Chicago, gift of Mrs Gilbert W.
Chapman in memory of Charles B.
Goodspeed, 1948.561, photo
copyright Art Institute of Chicago,
All Rights Reserved, picture
copyright Succession Picasso/DACS
1998

*Is anybody there? Personhood, the person with whom you can have eye to eye contact, is not
there; it has been vacuumed-away (or as postmoderns say, deconstructed), by the artist's reductive
perceptualizing. But something is there, hovering in this depleted space; some person-substitute
strong enough to stop one asking where reality has gone.* See pp. 113 and 130.

Plate 22
Hans Holbein
(1497/8–1543)
The Ambassadors, 1533
National Gallery,
London

Daylight floods the scene; the light of the New Learning, dispelling the darkness of church and academic tradition. Then as now, the new technology of science, and the arts, was presented as objects of faith; along with a Lutheran hymnbook, whose own securities the tools of learning were eventually to threaten; a half-hidden crucifix hints at an alternative confidence. See p. 94.

Plate 23 Francisco de Goya
(1746–1828)
Don Andres de Peral, exh 1798
National Gallery, London

Goya's artist colleague with the palsied face may not be as sinister as he looks; but his hard stare is not without a cruelty, even towards himself; the stoic refusal, by the modern era, of the salve of faith for the wounds of life. See p. 113.

Plate 24 Jackson Pollock (1912–1956)
No 1 1950, Lavender Mist National Gallery of Art, Washington, Ailsa Mellon Bruce
Fund, copyright Trustees, National Gallery of Art, Washington
Pollock's pictures seem to have almost physically changed since the fifties, from riotous aggression
to Old Masterish restraint, but there is still a world in there for those who care to enter; try it,
but check your exit.
See the 'thought experiment', 'Jackson Pollock and Hebrews', p. 122.

Plate 25 David Bomberg (1890–1957)
Jerusalem, towards Mount Scopus, 1925 Tate Gallery, London
A prodigious labour of colour and tone, focussed apparently on mere surfaces, but driven by the
intuition (artistic, more than religious), that harmony of surface has a meaning beyond chance.
See p. 137.

**Plate 26 Giovanni Bellini
(c 1430–1516)**
Portrait of Doge Loredano, 1501–4
National Gallery, London

Venice's helmsman through years of crisis, at the outset of his reign, dressed in the serenity of his willing service to 'La Serenissima', the Venetian state. See p. 131.

**Plate 27 Pieter de Hooch
(1629–after 1684)**
Courtyard of a House in Delft,
1658 National Gallery, London

Here is an art that makes connections; between light, space, and air; between old bricks, northern climate and human tread; between persons and the commonality of life under the sun; to be contrasted with the presentation of unmediated matter in some recent art, in which connections are not inherent, but have to be inferred. See p. 136.

Plate 28 Paul Hobbs (b1964)
Chorus, 1992 (acrylic on paper, 50cm x 65 cm) Private collection
An attempt to convey through layered colour and gesture something of the joy and vitality of Christian life; one of the virtues of this kind of art is that its spirit comes from inside and cannot be faked; and by authenticity to a whole approach to life, has staying power. See p. 160.

Plate 29 Richard Kenton Webb (b1959)
The Spoken Word, 1994 (oil on cotton, 159.5cm x 200cm) Collection: the artist
Here are spaces to get into - real finite ones, where the early Creation is alone and quiet with its maker, and his Spoken Word beams intelligence and perspective into the unformed waste - and pools of reflected gold hint at the beginnings of a response.

**Plate 30 Richard
Kenton Webb (b1959)**
The Dead Christ, 1988-9
Private collection

A short life finished; it should be the end of hope; yet it is more like the clear-up after the decisive performance is over; the poetry of sunset clothes the mourners, promising a better dawn.
See p. 160.

**Plate 31 Mark
Cazalet (b1964)**
Martha and Mary,
1995 Private
collection

Modern life is so busy; a lot of talk, and food to be got on the table, and someone is getting in the way trying to sort out her life with Jesus; a modern parable from two Bible stories.
See p. 160.

Plate 32 Mark Cazalet (b1964)
Sixth Hour, 1995 (141cm x 106cm)
Private collection

The title refers to the crucifixion, and the darkness which came for three hours (Matthew 27:45);
time telescopes to the present as tower blocks and graffiti silently witness God's love and blood.
See pp. 156 and 160.

Plate 33 Roger Wagner (b1957)
The Harvest is the End of the World And the Reapers are Angels, 1989 Private
collection
The clear, unearthly light seems to come from nearer than the sun, and angels about their work
are ominously impartial: a time of recognition, when relativism's last complaints will cease.
See pp. 160 and 162.

PART III

ART IN HISTORY: FROM PAGAN TO CHRISTIAN – AND BACK

I once had the privilege of looking round an art gallery with one of our leading restorers. We came to a picture by an artist whose work he specialized in. Knowing that restorers can see things that most of us miss, about the condition of paintings and the changes that have been made to them, I asked him whether that spoilt the art for him. 'Not at all', he replied. 'When I look at paintings for pleasure, I do not even notice their condition.' Something of the same may be said for the section of the book we are entering into. There are many ways of looking at paintings. The 'religious diagnostic' is by no means the only thing that can be said about them, and it is not appropriate all the time.

But that said, there are aspects to the history of art which require explanation. Many art history books still manage to portray the 'story of art' in unbroken sequence, as if it was a story of almost inevitable development and discovery. The constant, 'art', is somehow supposed to have survived unscathed through its gruelling historical ordeal. But as we have seen, there may be some very different things going on under the name of art.

So far, the assumption has usually been that the investment by modern artists in the art of 'primitive religions' has been largely formal; signifying, that is, a change in artistic but not religious commitments. It has also been assumed that the relationship between viewer and work of art in the modern period has not fundamentally changed. The viewer remains in charge. But if we are right about the 'personal dynamics of art', as in the last chapter, and if this century has seen something like a religious vacuum waiting to be filled – then these relationships are probably very different from those we had understood. Putting that together with the unprece - dented spiritual ingenuity of Picasso and his successors – we are probably not wrong to think that modern art is less purely about art than we had thought – and that we may need to redraw our maps.

Chapter Eight

Spiritual Energies of Modern Art

Watch out, there's a theory about[29]

I wonder whether theories make you as wary as they do me? When you are away from an experience, they seem very much in charge. You feel all the confidence of a policeman with an arrest-warrant in his pocket. But when you (as policeman) arrive at the man's front door, he has a disconcerting way of talking his way out of it. So it goes, frequently, when we try to arraign our experience of works of art armed with a theory. Too often, the art refuses to cooperate. We have to console ourselves with the thought that without the theory, we might not be there at all.

Therefore, before attempting to draw together some of the themes of the previous part, it is worth mentioning that a theory is a modest tool, a starting place for negotiations with the work of art, but by no means a substitute for them. Otherwise a broad theory has a tendency to take on a free-floating existence of its own, not unlike an idol itself, seeming to be very strong when in isolation, but becoming insubstantial as soon as it is asked to do any real work. Whereas what we should perhaps hope for a theory is to provide a hint, or a suggestion, to bring you to the boundaries of the thing discussed, after which you can, more or less, fend for yourself.

Here's the theory

The hint, or suggestion, is this. It is generally agreed that the last two centuries have been marked by what we may call 'subject-object tension'. The grand philosophical attempt dating from the Enlightenment to establish certain foundations for knowledge has led, almost at every passing decade, to less and less certainty that we can know anything. It is also agreed by many art historians that subject-object tension, usually

---

[29] The allusion is to a British poster campaign a few years back, 'Watch out, there's a thief about'. One does not usually notice the loss there is with a theory. But at least there is usually gain as well.

described as philosophical positivism,[30] has had profound implications for art. If the object cannot be known in its fullness, that would result in a sense of isolation for the subject (that is, the artist). The result is a more 'subjective' art, and a retreat from realism. This is one of a number of very general explanations for the twentieth-century move into 'non-objective art'. If you cannot know reality, there can be no inhibitions about making it up. This uncertainty starts to have important implications for metaphys - ics, and for our theme, idolatry. If you cannot know God reliably, there is nothing to stop you inventing him either. If you are an artist, that means imaging whatever you think 'the ultimate' to be. (You cannot know him, so you have made him.) Unfortunately, in the art history textbooks, this appears as a quite innocent occupation.

We have also seen that the Enlightenment's certainty-in-knowledge project itself had a spiritual implication. It is not just about knowledge, and it was not necessarily the only rational course to have taken. If reality was originally set up so that there is some kind of partnership between humans and God, then any desire to find ways of attaching meaning to nature, and guaranteeing knowledge of it, as an operation independent of God, looks rather odd. It is the epistemological equivalent of taking your cash from a cash machine rather than facing the lady at the till. There is something here about the pleasures of independence and the illusion of an unlimited account!

When Jesus told his story about the son who wanted independence, and took the cash and went, it was a picture, among other things, of the drive of humankind to become independent operators in creation. An essential part of that 'cash' is the sense of unrestricted access to reality by means of certain knowledge. And like the cash in the story, it did partly work. The certainty that had in fact come from an original belief in God (and which provided such essential foundations for science as a belief in a reliable, ordered cosmos) could indeed be operated independently of him, with spectacular results. This actually provided a new sense of self-confidence. There was talk, which even theologians at last came to agree with, of 'man having come of age'. But while we enjoy that sense of maturity, we are still not so good at understanding the point of the parable. We still define maturity in terms of independence. But in the story the son came back. He wanted to be a slave, but he was actually

---

[30] Such effects range from the apparently uncommitted factuality of early Impressionism, which G.H. Hamilton interprets as influenced by the scientific positivism of Auguste Comte (see Hamilton's *19th and 20th Century Art*, p. 100), to the more diffuse effects of the later logical positivism, with its disavowal of metaphysics. The critical point is where the integrating powers of a sole-scientific view of reality give way to the disintegrating consequences of metaphysical meaninglessness. See also, for its theological insight on Impressionism, T.F. Torrance, *The Ground and Grammar of Theology*, p. 32.

brought into partnership as a son. Suddenly there is a reversal. What had looked so 'adult', the attempt to get free from relationship and set up independently, begins to look childish. The adult is the one who comes back, who is content to find meaning in community, and to be a recipient rather than the supposed creator of knowledge. The adult is the one who finds everything returned to him. It is childish not to receive the meaning that is there.

Putting together the outward events of philosophical history (the 'subject-object tension' resulting from the Enlightenment project) with their inner story (a deliberate attempt to set up grounds of knowledge that are fully-functioning in independence of God), we come to the following result. If the centre of the whole exercise is the person's self, sitting in the circle of reality trying to prove its existence, and then worrying that what he has 'proved' is probably the creation of his own mind – there is not a great difference between the idea of knowledge as a set of human systems centred on the self, painted like constellations on the ceiling of his mind, and the attempt of the same self, defeated by that exercise, to create alternative universes. An idolatry of the individual mind moves quickly into an idolatry of what that mind can create.

So it is not difficult to see 'modernity', the tools of Enlightenment rationalism which have transformed the world, and 'modernism', the new art which has heralded the end of rationalism, as one whole event. There is admittedly the danger of an intellectual conceit here, as we are talking about two very different worlds. Goya is one kind of artist and Picasso another. Some thread that held reality to Goya, and Goya to reality, for Picasso has snapped. Despite the figuration of Picasso's work, his engagement with the great themes of life and death, sometimes in laughter, sometimes in rage, a certain confidence in dealing with the world has gone. And Picasso is a more world-attached artist than many. The argument is simply that although Enlightenment confidence and Enlightenment doubt produce different appearances, they have the same root.

See
Plate
23
See
Plate
21

We have therefore tentatively reached the conclusion that the Enlight - enment project, for an independently grounded basis for knowledge, was, in the first place liable to hinder (by doubt and self-consciousness) the normal ability to perceive, and therefore to depict, the world, and in the second place, that it was inherently idolatrous. Therefore there were two very strong engines for creating idols: one the necessity for subjective isolation, and two, the desire for it. We also discussed at length whether it is possible for works of art to actually be idols, in practice. We acknowledged an instinctive feeling that such an idea was grotesque, or at least grotesquely exaggerated. In response we argued that, constituted as we are, idolatry in art is the more likely option.

There is an unbreakable linkage between the beings and objects we worship, what we image, and what we try to be. Human beings, unlike flowers, cannot grow without having something to follow. We are pre-programmed to look up. In our heads, we must have an idea of what we want to be. Therefore it is quite possible that the images of art could be our personal mail-order catalogue for modelling our identity. We have then a convergence, of the fact that the new theory of knowledge knocked the bottom out of realism (philosophical and artistic), and the fact that the loss of belief in God that went with it created a new need for images. The likelihood is that functioning idols will be created. Is this then the story of modern art?

As I have said, watch out when there's a theory about, especially one as simple as that. The better the evidence, the more you have to worry! As a matter of fact, there is some evidence for this suggestion, of which more in a moment; but first, because we are dealing with something as important as a whole approach to modern art, there is something else we need to consider.

Hitler the art critic

Considering the company one is keeping, it is a very serious matter to make any sort of general criticism of mainstream twentieth-century art. It is impossible to forget that one of its foremost opponents was Hitler, who in the cause of his mission to 'purify' German art had thousands of modern works removed from museums. To show his thoroughness, he also ordered to be burnt over a thousand paintings and sculptures, and about four thousand works on paper, (as a fire-fighting 'practice exercise' by the Berlin Fire Department), and to make some money, he sold 126 works of the 'degenerate art' he had confiscated (including Van Gogh, Matisse, Picasso) by auction in Switzerland. In Germany, many artists were forbidden to sell, exhibit, or even to buy artists' materials. [31]

If this had been some campaign of mindless destruction it would be easier to understand. But the true horror of it lies in the principles in which the violence of the Nazis were clothed. Hitler's anger against modernism was, on the face of it, based on positive beliefs about what art should be, principles which sound not wholly unlike those which, we must admit, could very easily be labelled 'Christian'. In a speech inaugu - rating the 'Great Exhibition of German Art' in 1937, he set out his view that modern art was morally diseased, and that it had only gained a following because of media promotion: 'so-called art criticism' (in the 'Jewish' press, of course) had succeeded in 'confusing the natural concepts about the nature and scope of art . . . above all . . . undermining and destroying the general wholesome feeling in this domain'. He believed

---

[31] Details from Martin Gilbert, review in the *Times Higher Education Supplement*, January 20, 1995, p.21, of Lynn H. Nicholas, *The Rape of Europa: the Fate of Europe's Treasures in the Third Reich and Second World War*, Macmillan, London.

that art should be intelligible and not need its own art-propaganda to support it. What he wanted was an art 'beautiful and, above all, decent'; 'diligent, and thus, in the final run, competent', conveying, in short, a 'holy conscientiousness'. In the name of such principles he would 'wage an unrelenting war of purification against the last elements of putrefaction in our culture'.[32]

Hitler the demagogue understood very well how to use the language of bourgeois values to prettify his activities, but there is in the language of this former (and not talentless) artist something more like a personal crusade, as if by these judgements of his own he aimed genuinely to protect the German people from harm. He was asking for an art that was beautiful, intelligible, and national; all of which does sound a better idea than an art ugly, incomprehensible, and homogeneously international. One could put up very good 'Christian' grounds for such views. Or at least, one could until one saw the actual art that might result.

There is of course the minor matter of how, in Hitler's proposals, truth, goodness and beauty should come about. God has not designed a world in which such things can come from the barrel of a gun. Hitler's values fail the test of having a credible gospel to implement them. But the real issue for us is that Hitler's response to modern art makes such values themselves seem questionable. For some modernists, that may not be a problem. Truth, goodness and beauty might for them already belong to the world of fascism. But for the Christian, Hitler's abuse of that terminology to promote a vacuous art of German propaganda does at least force us to question how different from his artistic values are one's own.

The simple answer to Hitler is that truth, goodness and beauty can only be had if truth, goodness and beauty are there. In the society he was creating there was little of any of those to be had, which is why so much art had literally to be stolen from other countries, and why Hitler wanted an art essentially to cover up the moral poverty of his nation. The last thing he wanted was the great works of art which were being created to reveal it. There was truth of course, but it was truth come close, not the distant truth of the respected masters. It was truth so loud that even a bully would notice it.

Christian values, then, should not be the values of the cover-up. Christians, regrettably, have often been attracted to respectability as the cheaper alternative to repentance, and might easily be drawn to an art that disguises rather than reveals. But any real art must be genuine. If society is split in its relationship with art and nature, that is what is there; if it is trying to discard aspects of the human image, that is what is there, and it is a better starting point for being honest with ourselves and God, if we have an art which expresses what is going on. God cannot deal with a sham.

---

[32] Quoted in Chipp (ed.), *Theories of Modern Art*.

This is, in a way, the discovery of twentieth-century art. It is also why Victorian religious art, against which our century has reacted, can have such an eerie quality, expressing materialistic emptiness even while it asserts religious truth. When the tide of religious belief is running out, it is better not to pretend, to 'hold the form of religion without its power' (2 Timothy 3:5). After watching the tensions of unbelief produce the painful sincerity of much Victorian ecclesiastical work, it is with a sense of relief that we greet the frank godlessness of early twentieth-century art, with its freedom of escape, like the joyful exit of schoolboys confined too long in chapel. But better still, if it can be had, is the truth not just to the way we see things, but to the way things actually are.

The challenge of Hitler's art criticism, then, is this. A moral art is not to be desired if it is stuck onto an immoral mind. A moral art is not to be associated with any form of compulsion; if it is, it ceases to be moral. The horror story of the Nazis and modern art is a chastening lesson to all would-be moralists, and a reminder of the possible link-up, discussed earlier, between respectability and the demonic. However, does the fact that Hitler hated modern art completely exonerate it? Very nearly. Someone who hated people so much could not begin to see or appreciate the likeness of God in the creativity of Klee, and Nolde, and Dix, and other persecuted artists. Or to put it more strongly, the evil working through him did recognize it, and wanted to destroy it. Moreover his own perverted creativity, the false artist in him, could not tolerate the true artist in them, whose authenticity of being was bound up in a refusal to compromise with power.

But there is still the issue, which we have been raising at such length, not of what the modernist work is, but of what it does. In that area we need to have nothing to do with Hitler's criticisms. He found modern art unintelligible because he needed educating, as we all do. But perhaps as a religious charlatan with an eye to the competition, Hitler's reactions at least show the recognition of a spiritual power in modern art, a power which he knew could never be channelled into the delusory religion of Aryan uplift. We have no sympathy with the rivalry he felt, as an expert in power. But we are interested in the nature of the power he discerned; which from our point of view is better described not as competition with Hitler, but as a rivalry to Jesus.

The artist's promotion to legislator

Having warned ourselves against any desire to make persecutory state - ments against the generality of modernism, we can now turn our attention to the evidence.

An admirable description of the way modern art has developed is given in the standard work, *Painting and Sculpture in Europe 1880–1940*, by George Heard Hamilton. He is worth quoting, not just for his insights, but because he himself is a representative exponent of the self-image of his era. Writing first in 1967, Hamilton is still in the 'evangelistic' phase of modern art writing, in which he writes to open up modernism to the non-initiate. In his Introduction he explains the distinction between the older art where the public and the artist seemed to be on an equal footing, because both were operating against mutually accepted standards of representation, and the newer art, in which the artist invariably operated in advance of the public, presenting not only new perceptions but new languages of expression at the same time. He says that the spectator now has to follow where the artist leads. The spectator

> can no longer expect, as he had since the Renaissance, to be entertained by images passively presented to his eye . . . he has to become actively engaged with the work of art, he has had to accommodate his most recalcitrant visual habits to new forms and new ways of seeing forms. [33]

Hamilton is perhaps exaggerating the passivity of representational art, which has always needed an active mind for its appreciation, but he has not exaggerated the extreme adaptive engagement required of us by the innovative artist. Looking at modern art is a process of continual conversion and repentance out of fixed habits.

We have, then, a shift in power relations between artist and public. Now it could be argued that this process merely reflects and exemplifies the atomizing into personal subjectivity of value judgements which has taken place throughout society. 'The public' may not be able to judge art, but no more has it any right to judge any other area of private belief, such as sexual ethics, religious truth, or even, in extreme examples, standard spelling and pronunciation. Art is a matter of private belief, and since there are no such things as universal public truths on which public scrutiny may base its judgements, the public has to defer to the artist. As Hamilton puts it:

> Value judgements no longer have any relevance to generally accepted systems of aesthetics or artistic evaluation. . . Each new development requires a new aesthetic, or at least the revision of an earlier one, and the establishment of values is now the business of the artist. . . For some time this subjective, intensely personal bias was the principal source of conflict between a public which still looked for recognisable images of persons, places, and things, and the artist who was providing images of hitherto unimagined events . . . and of events occurring in newly invented spaces. [34]

---

[33] Hamilton, *Painting and Sculpture in Europe*, p. 17
[34] Ibid., pp. 16–17.

The artist was operating, so it seemed, as a subjective individual, and the public had no rights over him. 'Subjective', however, only has meaning where there are objective states to compare it with. But as Hamilton shows, calling the new art 'subjective' was merely a temporary, defensive phase while the new art was being adjusted to. What became clear before very long was that the old 'objective' centre was gone:

> the public also lost the very kind of art it most demanded. In the traditional forms of portraiture, mural painting for religious or govern - mental purposes, and genre painting the period . . . is all but barren'. [35]

Therefore that put the artist's leadership no longer at the margins of society, as a critic or alternative voice, but at the centre. The artist becomes a serious contributor to the creation of values.

This is where we begin to see the work of art as being given official recognition as occupying something like a religious role in society. Values no longer come handed down from a religious source as having other-worldly authority, but it is now the artist whose work evinces that special ability to perceive ultimates, and who is therefore invested with that personal authority. As Hamilton writes, with an almost embarrassing frankness:

> What seems to be emerging now, especially among the younger members of the public, is an understanding of art as a fundamental, constitutive, and essential factor in society – as a good in and of itself *– and of the artist as an acknowledged legislator of our spiritual, even of our political, condition.*[36]

The artist has, then, finally arrived, after humble beginnings as mere technician to the rich, at the exalted status as society's legislator. Before we work up too much shock, it is worth asking ourselves honestly whether this is such a bad thing. Modern artists have proved that they can teach things. Their canvases, and the far less conventional structures that they have pioneered, have stayed the course. Published and re-published in art books, many once-derided images have proved able to survive the ordeal of constant repetition. It is the public that has had to shift, rather than the producer. Consumer is not king here. If the public has shown it can listen, and the artist has made it listen, is it so unjust to allow the artist a special status as public seer?

Surely it is the artist, the musician, the poet, who tells us what life is like. It is the artist who, time and again, has learned to listen to society's cry, rather than, with the politicians, to stuff its mouth with

---

[35] Ibid., p. 17.

[36] Ibid., my italics.

the pacifying dummy of short-term comforts. It is the artist who takes the pain of life and refuses the anaesthetic. It is the artist who, while others are sealed inside, sticks his head out of the train window, and faces wind and smoke to try to see where it is going. The artist, then, is that serious person who takes time to feel and think, and to whom society might well be wise to entrust its soul. Here is the gospel of art. The artist is truthful; everyone else (almost) is a hypocrite. Trust the artist, the 'acknowledged legislator of our spiritual, even of our political, condition'.

Two gospels?

Make no mistake, the truthfulness of art is something very good about it, and the truthfulness of artists, following their light and not bending to crude commercial pressure, is something for which we need to be grateful. The product which society receives from artists may be unappetizing, indigestible, or downright poisonous, but on the whole, it appears to be trustworthy.[37] To have created an art-culture in which what is genuine thrives, in these times of uncertain values, is no small feat. But is the genuineness of modern art enough to constitute a gospel?

What is at stake here is nothing small. We underrate both the position of contemporary art and its quality if we think 'gospel' is simply a metaphor for 'rather good', and to be placed in shy inverted commas. The claim of modern art to be gospel is based on no less than the claim that artists have the ability to see and to know where others do not, and that they can transmute what they know into art. Art therefore gives the access which society needs to truth. That would indeed be good news (gospel). In a world deprived of publicly given, institutionally validated, ultimate truths, art can, apparently, provide not just mental but sensory experience of the truths we need to live. Open-mouthed like chicks in a nest, we hunger for the food the artist brings. Society knows its need. The gospel of art says that our need can be satisfied.

But what of the other gospel, which, by now, may have modestly retired into the shadows? At this point, perhaps without realizing it, we have reached a fork in the road. We must make choices. Can the artist really find the knowledge we need from within the world? Everything depends on what we understand by truth, and how much truth we believe is accessible to us without external help.

---

[37] Sometimes, reading the art press, I wonder if I am being naïve. Gimmicks, media manipulation, and every other trick of marketing, possibly abound in contemporary art; but what I am trying to portray is the thread of integrity, even integrity to ideas I consider false, that gives some kind of structure to the whole process.

There is a plausible case for the gospel of art being true, but only on certain conditions. If the world is indeed, as many believe in the West, a closed system, and the only knowledge we can have is what we perceive, then indeed we should tune in to the most sensitive receptors. If those are the artists, we should tune into them, though not forgetting comple - mentary forms of knowledge. If it is true that life is what we feel it to be, then we must allow our most powerful feelers to describe it for us. If artists are the only seismographs of reality, let us use them. And if it is true that what seems right to a man is what is good, by all means let some of our most genuine citizens legislate for us. If this is the land of the blind, then let us make the one-eyed artist king. Better the truth we can get through art than no truth at all. If the centre has gone, by all means let us listen to the edges.

However, suppose that the world is not a closed system. Suppose that the state of 'being in touch' that we crave is possible, in a more absolute sense than art could ever provide; absolute because it is validated from outside? The weakness of art is that there is always the doubt that it is we, in cosy self-reference, who are providing the validation.

But what if truth came to us as fully accredited, in a way that was independent of us? This is what the Christian faith claims has already happened.

> God who at sundry times and in divers manners spake in time past . . .
> hath in these last days spoken to us by his Son . . . by whom also he
> made the worlds . . . (Hebrews 1:1–2, AV)

God spoke, God has spoken, and to do so he has sent the top man, the one to whom he has confided his knowledge and through whom he made, not just this problematic little world, but 'the worlds', including all the ones our sci-fi mad generation is not even speculating about. So we have access to 100 per cent genuine knowledge. That would be a gospel worth hearing about.

But this raises an obvious question. Does the external source of truth (God speaking) conflict with the kind of truth that artists can discern for us from within the system? Otherwise, there is plainly no need to choose. Both gospels could function at the same time. Is God the creator saying different things through the Scriptures and in the person of his Son than can be plainly read from his Creation? Not surprisingly, this is a slightly delicate matter to answer. We do not expect God to lie through his creation; but neither do we expect that he would tell us everything. There could be more to say. And the more that he could tell us in person might well transform our understanding of what we had discovered for ourselves.

The idea that there could be more hinges on the fact of a personally present God wanting to have something to do with us. A child who was given a present might be satisfied with it, and indeed preoccupied with it, but he would not for that reason desire the parent-giver to be dumb. The gift does not supplant the giver: their functions are quite different. The child knows that there are also higher levels of giving from the parent (e.g. contact, play, plans), some of which might transform the terms in which the present is seen. What we think of as the whole becomes very different when we see it is just the part. This is all beside the fact that some of our understanding of the gift, without explanation from the giver, might actually be wrong. Unlike the child of a busy parent, given something to 'occupy' it while the parent was elsewhere, we might never have been intended to use and understand the gift on our own.

But this is very abstract. We need to try a thought experiment. What we want to see is this: how does the world look when seen, by an artist, from within the world as a closed system; and how does that same view appear when seen alongside the gospel of Christ? Does the gospel affirm the truths which art has discovered? Does it contradict, transform, or relegate them to a lower level? How does it change our sense of the reliability of the artist's perceptions? I am taking as an example one of the masters of American abstract painting.

Thought experiment: Jackson Pollock and Hebrews

Stage one. Some readers will have seen Jackson Pollock's big drip paintings in actuality, an experience which may or may not have been overwhelm - ing, depending as it does on one's state of mind, the tiredness of one's feet, or more subtle things like philosophical openness. The size is important, in that you need to stand close or imagine yourself doing so, to become immersed in the jungle of hanging and rising skeins of paint, as if in a nature of the artist's own making. Sometimes you cannot see it at all. I will admit to having spent many hours at close range unable to see what the fuss was about. Later on I recognized the world that was in the paintings. For those that are sceptical about such as Pollock, it is as well not to rely on my descriptions, but to enter into the experience of his classic works as beautifully described by a leading scholar of Abstract Expressionism. My aim here is to begin with a 'neutral' experience of Pollock, unhindered, that is, by Christian thought.

The writer likens the balance in Pollock's 'classic' period to a certain moment in Greek art:

> As applied to fifth-century BC Greek art, 'classical' denotes a peak when chaos was mastered and extremes balanced and it is this same poise about [Pollock's] 1947–50 images [e.g. *Lavender Mist*, Washington, National Gallery] that allows them to reconcile contradictions. Empty of imagery, they feel intensely full; lacking overt references to nature, the organic patterns of growth nevertheless engulf us; rather

See
Plate
24

monochromatic overall, strong and metallic hues shimmer through their interstices; heavy with the quiddity of paint, their space floats and dances in front of one's eyes.[38]

Pollock's own remark, 'I don't paint nature, I am nature' confirms the sense that Anfam describes of being engulfed in the organic world of a Pollock, as if the assumed boundaries between ourselves and nature were being dissolved. You cannot 'walk into' a Pollock, in the sense of occupying space as something distinct from that space, partly because the hanging tangle of paint is, as it were, in your way. Instead the paintings evoke a sense of entering in by a process of identification, of becoming one with the organic world described. By the process of identity, the experience is of being simultaneously inside and outside the work.

From this either first-hand or second-hand experience, two conclu-sions should be drawn at this stage. First, that these are genuine works of art, conveying something real, a perception that can be entered into; and second, that this perception is of an immediate and sensory nature. It is of the order of 'this is what life, the world, seems or feels to be like'. The fact that we as viewers can empathize with the experience gives it something of a universal quality. The question is: *if this is what life feels like, is it what life is actually like?*

Thought experiment stage two. Remember, if the world is a closed system, the only knowledge we have is that of investigative science (count it) and of the arts (feel it). But here we are going to see if subjective understanding can be corrected by the application of knowledge from outside.

So here I am, in a gallery looking at Pollock, and I decide to wash my vision down with a treatment of the gospel, of the definitive idea-frame that purports to come from outside the system by the one who began it, continues it, and will wrap it up. Almost at random, I find myself reading a version of the gospel in the letter to the Hebrews. I have read it before, but this time I am reading it in relation to Pollock: the impact will be two-way.

At the place I begin, the unknown author is quoting from Psalm 8, and speaking about the nature of the human:

But one in a certain place [i.e. in the psalm] testified, saying, 'what is man, that thou art mindful of him? or the son of man, that thou visitest him?

'Thou madest him a little lower than the angels; thou crownest him with glory and honour, and didst set him over the works of thy hands: thou hast put all things in subjection under his feet.' (Hebrews 2:6–7, AV)

---

[38] David Anfam, *Abstract Expressionism*, p. 130.

As I enter into what Hebrews says, I am already starting to pull back from the experience of the Pollock. Hebrews tells me I am 'crowned with glory and honour': I am given a substantial identity from outside. I enter nature already 'crowned', by which I understand that, since I have not crowned myself, it is God himself (as the psalm says) who has placed value upon me, and made me someone of worth. For some reason which perhaps I do not yet understand, this sense of worth gives me less desire to merge with nature. I do not need to, I have substance already.

The psalm has then gone on to say that, far from being engulfed by nature, it has been put 'in subjection' under my feet, a point which the writer amplifies:

For in that he put all in subjection under him, he [that is, God] left nothing that is not put under him [that is, man]. (verse 8)

Now we, of course, can immediately think of aspects of nature, such as volcanoes and tornadoes, that cannot possibly be said to be in subjection to man. This is where 'external revelation' begins to cut across subjective experience.

Subjective experience tells us that, despite centuries of effort to take charge of nature, some of which we are starting to regret, it is by no means under our feet. We might very well, based on experience alone, go along with Pollock's view and say in effect, 'if you can't beat it, join it'. We could excuse ourselves by thinking that the author of Hebrews was, in the main, referring to the human position, or status in relation to nature, rather than nature actually being under our authority in a practical sense. It is true that the writer's aim is to say something about how God values man; but he goes on to ensure that we see that the value God puts on man is meant to have practical, visible, results. For he makes this laconic comment:

But now we see not yet all things put under him. (verse 8)

The word 'yet' introduces us to the idea that the subjective experience of nature that we have, though perfectly reliable as far as it goes, is not the complete story. The true position of human kind is not 'yet' seen for what it is. In fact, from the visible evidence, you would not guess what the true position of humans was.

But, because this is gospel, (actual news, with something tangible to take hold of), there is after all some physical evidence, though often-overlooked, of what humanity is:

But we see Jesus. (verse 9)

So now the focus is on Jesus. He is the window onto the present, but not yet fulfilled, state of affairs. He is the one we must see, as our exemplary man, walking into Pollock's jungle. But when we look at Jesus, what do we see? Do we not see him as like ourselves, subject to nature, but more so: bleeding and thirsting, nailed on a cross of wood under a fierce sun and left to die? Or is there something else as well?

> But we see Jesus, who was made a little lower than the angels for the suffering of death, crowned with glory and honour; that he by the grace of God should taste death for every man.

The writer does not tell us quite what he 'sees' when he sees Jesus crowned with glory and honour. We have to guess. There is something of elevation about the resurrection: a freedom from all that nature was able to do; as if the shame of the cross had also included the shame of the Lord of life yielding to the physical. But in the resurrection there is now the glory of a new humanity, that neither death, nor space, nor gravity could hold.

Now 'we see Jesus', as the one who both authenticates our experience of life (he has gone through the mill of nature that we know), and who de-authenticates it at the same time. He shows us that our experience is no longer absolute or definitive: it neither shows us how things should be, or shall be. Jesus even gives a hollowness to the rigidities of how we suppose things are. This is because he has 'tasted death', not just for himself but for everyone – by which we understand that the primacy of the natural order has been undermined, its teeth have been removed, it can bite but not eat. Therefore anyone who still subjects himself to it does so not because he is absolutely bound to, but by his (religious) volition. The world has changed, in prospect but also in essence. This is something that artists would need to know about.

Thought experiment stage three. We have now charged our minds with the news from outside the closed system, news which has a radical bearing on how we see nature. 'What you see is what you get' is true of nature if you care to leave things that way, but any spiritual primacy mere matter may have had over us has gone. A new human position, which actually fulfils our essential nature, is now available. How does Pollock look now?

I have been looking at a Pollock reproduction intermittently while writing the above, and I have found its appearance to be strangely changeable. Sometimes *Lavender Mist* has been looking like a scored mud-flat seen from close range, sometimes like an aerial photograph of bombarded cities. In all the changes there seems to be one constant, which is that the more I meditate on the revelation of Jesus, the greater grows the painting's density and opacity. The original sense of a living surface of transparent veils is lost, and the paint come to cohere into a solid mass, which is no longer living, but more like the detritus of a life. I no longer find myself entering in (that is, the 'I' that I find myself to be when more fully clothed with Christ), but see it much more from the outside: a visual parallel to all things being 'in subjection' under my feet. I also feel less sense of identity with the actions of the artist. The rhythmic and dynamic spatter and run of paint is no longer 'me', and executed for me. Next to the glory of Jesus, it seems much more clearly to be the expression of Pollock's mind and Pollock's world, both of which seem limited. Instead of seeing Pollock introducing me to an endless expanse of 'nature', I see Pollock not in infinity but boxed in, the marks on canvas looking like the frenzied trails of a rat in a run.

The art-loving reader will not thank me for a religious experience whose main outcome seems to be the ruination of a good picture. But I suppose it is less important that a picture is ruined than a person. Our commitments do matter. What if we enter into the 'infinity' of Pollock's nature, and stay there, not realizing that it is in fact a box with no exit? It is more useful to us to be on the outside of it, with the knowledge that nature is not all there is.

It may also be wondered whether, in my own subjectivity, I am being fair to Pollock. As it happens, we can corroborate what we think we see in the paintings with what we know of his religious beliefs:

> An aversion to conventional religion hid a search for wholeness. At an early stage ideas from such fashionable sources in California then as theosophy and Krishnamurti guided him towards lifelong pantheism . . . [39]

Pantheism, the idea that identifies God with nature, obviously leaves no room for there to be anything beyond nature. There are no bigger spaces, there is no one to 'crown' us with glory and honour, or to set us 'over the works of [his] hands'. There is therefore no possibility of redemption which, by definition, does for us what we cannot do for ourselves. Nor is there any possibility of love, either of God or of Nature, because there can be no love where there is no distinction. Trying to bring the concept of love into a Pollock highlights something brittle and alien about his suspended interwoven coils.

Not two gospels, then

Our thought experiment shows that artists who were only reliant, however truthfully, on what nature disclosed to them, might well come up with a view with which the gospel of Christ conflicts. But it also shows that that gospel does not require us to refuse the evidence of our senses. It actually shows us better what is there. And by contrast it shows up the view that has not been instructed from outside as sensorily inadequate.

It is the gospel which points up the possibilities in nature for relation - ship, and which therefore enables us to see it in a concrete and distinct

---

[39] Anfam, p. 30.

way (that is, the way of love). This is deepened when we see, through the gospel, that the relationships of love are based in a hierarchy: God, humankind and nature.[40] (That is to say, the relationships are unequal, but that does not preclude the giving and receiving of love.) From knowing what should be there, we can see better what actually is there.

Most importantly, the gospel accounts for a feature of nature which Pollock's account is trying to suppress, because it can by no means explain it. This is the acute ambivalence we feel about the sense of authority in respect of nature which is our instinctive birthright (and responsibility), and the frustration we have, because of our inability to get outside nature's system. Pollock's pantheistic solution is to turn the sense of being helplessly embodied within the frame of nature into a virtue, thus abolishing the sense of loss. He smothers the sense of lost pre-eminence by denying it. It is like solving the problem of authority in the classroom by pretending the teacher is one of the kids. There may be a short-term sense of relief for the teacher! But frustration and loss will surface. Likewise, reality outside Pollock's paintings eventually has to be faced. The cloud of knowing will evaporate.

Pollock longed, we are told, to find wholeness; but the world as it presents itself to us never can be fully coherent. The gospel is not an addition to a satisfactory picture, but the answer to a state of affairs which, on the face of it, is contradictory. The promised glory of man and the taste of death are, as every bereaved person knows, grotesquely opposed. But with the gospel we have in Adam the explanation, and with Jesus the solution. The outside answer to nature transforms it on the inside.

★ ★ ★

There is no need to repeat our thought experiment with other artists to see that we cannot, after all, rely on what artists are telling us. The fork in the road turns out to be more important than perhaps we had realized. The fork offering us *the gospel of art* is now seen to be a cul-de-sac, in which only false solutions can be offered to the conundrum of life. Even heroically hopeless solutions, as, say, Rothko's appear to be, are found to be hermetically misinformed. Nature in itself, so full of promise, though it proves nothing, is shown to be the better guide. But if we take the fork of the real gospel, *the gospel of Christ*, that turns out not to take us out of this reality, but to flood it with light and significance. When Jesus ascended into heaven, he had cleared up the existential nightmare with which our supposedly well-informed artists are still wrestling.

---

[40] For discussion of the virtues of hierarchy as a structure that enables freedom, see Chapter 3, Natural Art.

Chapter Nine

Modern Art's Working Invention

When looking at the Jackson Pollock, we have seen it as one possible way of looking at the world. In that way, it does not differ from most 'conventional' works of art, with the difference that, instead of becoming a lens through which to look at the world, it can start to function as an alternative world, accessed through the mind. But we can still see his view as having a defined 'content', and say 'this was how Pollock saw things'.

In this chapter, we need to look at an invention of modern art which is a little more complex. The advantage, or the 'problem', of defined content, is that we can always compare it with the reality we have. It means that the work of art can never be its own authority, and the artist can never be her own authority. That, as we have laboured to say, is a good fact about art in Creation, even if artists chafe against it. It is something which defends the work of art from getting too self-important, by standing outside this Creation, and it defends the viewer from having to take it entirely on trust. But there is an invention of art which, I believe, has discovered a way to circumvent this 'problem'; and to give works of art, and their creators, the authority which had been denied them. In spiritual terms, this invention has a capacity for acting as an idol, but in such completely modern dress that only its influence could give us any confirmation that it has done so. The invention is Cubism, and its various successors.

Conceptual art and negative concepts

But first, some brief clarification may be needed on the subject of 'conceptual' art. I mean 'conceptual' in the terms of the early part of the century, not the conceptual installation art of today, which is almost exclusively idea-based. It might be thought that our baseline is in fact visual representation, and that what we find questionable is the move to a more symbolic, less realistic imagery. But we are not talking here about the twentieth century's move from a strictly visual, to a more idea-based descriptive art. Picasso said, 'I paint forms as I think them, not as I see them'.[41] When he painted a portrait of Françoise Gilot as a flower, he was

---

[41] Hamilton, *Painting and Sculpture in Europe*, p. 15.

trying to convey as much how he thought of her, as how he saw her. He, and others like him, were strongly influenced by the 'conceptual' images of children. This is simply a neutral fact about modern art, with no necessary spiritual significance: we can paint symbols, or we can paint representations, and both have a purpose. Eastern Orthodox painting, like medieval art, is largely conceptual rather than visual and spatial. A symbolic as well as a visual language can convey a Christian conception of the world, as many living Christian artists, who are benefiting from this revolution of modern art, are finding.

There is, in any case, no strict division between visual and conceptual, until we get down to words. And both can have strong reference to the world outside. What is important in Cubism, which is a kind of visual-conceptual hybrid, is the ingenious way in which the referent of the picture is kept within the picture space.

Cubism

In launching such an interpretation of Cubism, we need to ask whether, as with Jackson Pollock, what we think we see finds any resonances in the writings of some of the standard histories, and also whether 'normal' explanations are really adequate to what we find. My own initial experi - ence of Cubist paintings, which has been confirmed as I have talked to others, is of works of great strength and intellectual resolve, but whose power and significance seems to lie perplexingly outside themselves. It is the 'having been done' which is important, rather than the pleasure they give now. Many of the great classics of art, from any age, 'go on giving'; but with Cubist works, it is as if their energy has given out. They are both immensely powerful monuments, and oddly ignorable. This experience squares well with the 'idol thesis', which is that these works function more by what they do, than what they are.

The question which Cubist paintings pose concerns their relationship to their subject matter. Indeed, what is the point of their subject matter? All manner of theories have been proposed. But we have to start with the priority of the paintings, the fact that, however difficult to explain, they do make some sort of sense. There are perhaps two initial lines of interpreta - tion, when we confront these dis-representational representations. They come under the headings of 'less' (of the real world) and 'more'.

a) The 'less' aspect of Cubism
In the light of the philosophical events we have discussed, it seems likely that the collapse, indeed the implosion inside the picture space, of purely representational art was due to a collapse in meaning. If that is the case, representation being devalued, a new conceptual art might have been devised which does not have equivalent meaning to pure representation, but creates its own meanings. This was in fact the view propagated by the

Cubist theorists, Gleizes and Metzinger, who, in George Heard Hamil -
ton's account, are quoted as typifying the new movement. They make a
sharp distinction between the doubtful nature of sensory perception, and
the certitude offered by mental imagery (which, of course, is not certitude
in respect of anything outside itself).

> A realist will fashion the real in the image of his mind . . . Far be it
> from us to throw any doubts upon the experience of objects which
> impress our senses; but rationally speaking, we can only experience
> certitude in respect to the images they produce in our minds. [42]

In other words, the new Cubist artist can be certain of what he makes,
but he cannot have any certainty that it refers to anything. This is
completely consistent with Cubist practice, in which objects and people
are recognizable, but certainly not with the purpose of giving information
about them. It is the picture, not the object, that is the subject. Guitar or
bottle, for all that their particulars matter, might as well be a word; and
the words used on Cubist paintings, for all their meaning signifies beyond
a certain playful humour, might as well be patterns of paint. The world
out there has not ceased to exist, but it has ceased to impinge, or at least
to have any definite claim on us.

Here, then, we have an intelligible account of Cubism as a withdrawal
from sensory perception: the scrambled vision actually means 'less' of the
world we know, on the grounds that it cannot be known. Priority is given
to the world 'in here'. But here the suggestion (of Gleizes and Metzinger)
is that that world actually represents 'more'. The argument is that there
has been a trade-off. Less representation means more of something else.
So, does it? What exactly is the status of the world going on in the artist's
head, and now symbolically revealed in his picture?

b) The 'more' aspect of Cubism

A second line of argument, typified by one of Cubism's early art-historical
apologists, is that the artist has found a route to a greater reality than the
merely visual can disclose. As Douglas Cooper writes:

> The basic intention of Cubism was not merely to present as much
> essential information as possible about figures and objects but to
> recreate visual reality as completely as possible in a self-sufficing,
> non-imitative art form. [43]

In Cooper's interpretation we find reflected, I think, the longstanding
debate in art between 'general' and 'particular' nature, in which he has

---

[42] Ibid., pp. 15–16.
[43] Douglas Cooper, *The Cubist Epoch*, p. 49.

taken hold of the idea (Platonic and Aristotelian) that the real reality is more in the abstract 'substance' of an object, than in the particulars of nature that you actually see. Particular nature is simply the local, and varied form, of something more important, the universal. The 'real' plane tree is not the one you see, but the perfect form, of which you are only seeing an instance. Indeed the classical tradition in art, represented by such as Raphael, Poussin, Reynolds, and David, had tried to solve the Aristotelian problem of the particular and the universal, by suppressing the particular, the accidents of nature, in favour of the general and the generalized.

As I see it, the Christian understanding of creation has never had such a problem with the particular (the particular tree, the individual person), seeing it as valid in its own right, and not merely as an instance of the universal. By contrast it could be that Cubism does represent the attempt to arrive at some more solidly grounded and universal truth than visual appearances can disclose. One can almost persuade oneself, looking at Cubist paintings, and believe that they have got more 'reality' in them than one can see; a hidden, de-particularized 'substance'. The idea of getting inside form, rather than being limited to a particular local viewpoint, is attractive, theoretically. But it depends on there being some kind of inner substance to arrive at. And it also depends on the (actually illusionist) idea that the purpose of a work of art is to re-create form, rather than simply to refer to it. Oddly it makes Cubism more concerned with representation than representational art ever was.

Views such as Cooper's make good explanations of what Cubist pictures might be aiming to do; but it is a different matter to assert that 'recreating' the substance of 'visual reality' is what they actually succeed in. We have to make a Platonic leap of faith to believe that what is out there can be scrambled and pictorially reconstructed, and thereby have a greater 'substance' than the reality we have. Dissolve the essentialist mystery, and as collections of 'essential information', Cubist pictures are, on those terms, remarkably poor. You would certainly have difficulty recognizing any of the props depicted in them in a junk shop. Does this matter? But what else can 'essential information' mean? Likewise, the celebrated portrait of Picasso's dealer friend, Kahnweiler, hardly gives enough information, beyond a certain disjointed caricature, to recognize him by. Of course, it is remarkable that anything of him survives the Cubist treatment, which no doubt is why its realism is so greatly applauded, and it is so often treated as if its 'less' was 'more'. But surely some common sense is permitted. Unless Picasso and Braque were living on another planet to ours, their pictures cannot claim to be about reality.

See Plate 21

c) Cubism's other agenda

I do not think, then, that the accounts we have had so far really explain what makes a Cubist painting succeed, unless that it is intended to work up a *belief* that we are seeing 'more' rather than 'less'. However the clue to a possible third way of looking at them is in Cooper's phrase 'self-sufficing'. The Cubists aimed at a 'self-sufficing, non-imitative art form'. A *non*-self-sufficing art form, presumably, is a dependent one.

It had of course been good enough for art to be dependent, for hundreds of years, if not since its inception. A cave painting is depend - ent, in that it gains its point from the reality referred to: it is enjoyable because we see 'through' it to bison, and deer, and the other denizens of the cave-occupiers' world. It is dependent, too, in that (possibly) it had some other functionality beside enjoyment, though visual pleasure in the animal creation is certainly evident in it. A portrait of the Doge of Venice by Bellini is likewise dependent: far from standing alone, it claims partnership with us in the screne investigation of a human being. Knowing something about the real world of ducal power will no doubt add to our understanding of the painting. We should have been deprived of an entry into that reality if the painting had pretended to be 'self-sufficing'. But it had no need to be, because the artist was in no doubt that he lived in a shared reality, as one participant with a certain gift, operating as a gate to the world which it took others, with the complementary gift of understanding his art, to walk through. A self-sufficient work of art, in such a context, would have been pointless and useless.

See Plate 26

What is so special about the Cubists that they must now make 'self-sufficient' works of art? The explanation presumably lies in the historical moment. The new development which they face is the crisis in perception (as in the quotation from Gleizes and Metzinger); against this the artists boldly pitch their creativity. That which the rest of the world has lost, the artists have not lost, because they can create. Creativity is now seen by way of opposition to reality, or as a substitute for it, rather than in partnership with it. The attempt to connect to a referent is seen as naïve and futile: something Cooper is pleased to call the 'eye-fooling illusion of three-dimensional seeing', as opposed to the knowledge of the 'solid tangible reality of things'. It is this the artist is gifted to know about, it seems without the use of his eyes; the artists have their own hot-line to the real world.

There is nothing the matter with creativity being used independently of perception. Some Christian writers have suspected it is inherently arrogant for artists to try to create on their own, as if that was infringing the prerogative of God. There may be, as we shall see, a kind of art in which artists actually do, unconsciously, try to infringe God's prerogative, by attempting works of pure, first-order creation. But ordinary creativity, pattern making, abstract design and so forth, is a harmless, indeed healthy reflection of our being made in God's image. However Cubism, and the kind of art we are considering, does not seem to be creativity for the sake of it, of that kind.

As has often been pointed out, the remarkable feature of Cubism is the way in which it drew back from abstraction. It needed the content, the remnant of the subject matter on which it was based. Why did subject matter have to be there? We have looked at the explanation that it was because the Cubists were seriously grappling with the inner reality of their subjects, to 'penetrate to the inner structure of things'. But we have seen that this is not something we can actually test. We might, with Cooper, believe it to be so. We can look at Cubist paintings and find ourselves thinking that through them we can apprehend more than we can see. But there are, by definition, no external checks. The external route to reality has been lost, because the visible, or our perception of the visible, has been found wanting. So what, to return to our original question, is the status of the imagery? If it is not something we can establish as 'real', what is it?

The creation of 'not-reality'

The answer seems to lie around that 'not', and the transformation that it produces in our relations with the picture and the artist. The pictures are not 'somethings', as Cooper optimistically believed, but they work by being 'not somethings', *for which the original subject matter has to be there, in order to be denied*. When we look at Cubist paintings in detail, we find a consistent logic of 'denial', by which any thing which seems about to be something, a tangible form in three dimensions, is 'denied', by some strokes of the brush, which either bring it up to the surface, or push it down into the shallow picture-space. The argument continually is: 'we have the picture, not the thing'; but we do not have abstraction from the thing, because the meaning of the picture is in the 'not-thing'. This is where the pictures start to have their peculiar power.

Note how our relationship with the artist starts to change, because we can no longer make our own valid comparisons with the external world. We are confined either to the route that the artist has found (his personal periscope out of this reality to the Platonic world of the forms), or, to what is in effect a new reality of the artist's own making. But this is not a world of new created objects, which we could put alongside, and within, this present world. It is an altogether new world of 'not-reality', as if there were cracks in this present order of Creation. The reason that skeletons of representational life still remain in Cubist works is that they are the sign of the de-naturing of perception, as a persuasive invitation to the artist's own special-knowledge (gnostic is the technical word) perception. There is something 'real' here after all, but it is the artist's own 'reality'.

What does it do to us when we start to believe, even for a moment, that the artist can access a world other than our world? Such a belief may not make logical sense; but it could nevertheless be part of the experience of Cubist paintings, that the artist is party to a knowledge of the real reality, which I cannot be party to. It certainly is part of the art-historical myth, that Cubist paintings mysteriously convey a greater 'analysis' of their subjects than visual study, or indeed science, could reveal. The conse-quence of such a belief is to open up quite a large tear in the canopy of the real, perceptible, created world, because it presents the concept of privileged knowledge (the old word for this was priesthood), and of another, perhaps alternative system of values, accessible for those who are 'in the know'. This then does something to the world of values which, heretofore, we might have seen as universally true, and as accessible to all. It threatens it. Indeed it relativizes it. And it reduces the God of Creation to the status of god only of the perceptible world, not of the 'real world' of Cubist knowledge. If he is not god there, he is, in effect, not God at all.

'The artist knows best what is real', sounds odd stated baldly, but as a doubt, hanging around ordinary perception, it may have been surprisingly potent. I am returning to the question of the power of the pictures. It is not exactly an artistic power. You do not come away from a Cubist work with your perception of the world enriched, in the way that Chardin and Cézanne bring the world more into focus. But the power of thinking that the artist 'knows' may have had enormous repercussions outside the paintings.

Something, for example, happened in the world of architecture at or around the inception of modernism, to effectively deprive the non-specialist of the normal means of judgement. 'What you think is there is not what is actually there, because the specialist can see things you cannot see'. I do not wish to be misunderstood as issuing a blanket disapproval of the achievements of modernism, which I have benefited from as much as everyone else: light, clarity of form, freedom of invention. But it can hardly be denied that with modernism has entered a universal licence to construct in public spaces without any but the most casual reference to visual principle, a licence frequently excused on the grounds of aesthetic relativism, or that 'the expert knows best'. The way such a revolution, a real revolution in art, as Cubist painting, might have helped bring about that subjugation of the public mind, has nothing to do with direct visual influence. It is that those paintings really do engender a belief that perhaps there might be another, authentic way of seeing things: inaccessible to me, of course, but out there, 'someone knows'; so I surrender my judgement, and take what I am given (relativistic values) on trust.

We need to register what an odd exchange has taken place. Until the invention of Cubism and its derivatives, we had a 'dependent' art, in which canvases, for all that they referred dependently to the world outside, were full, reflecting the many splendours and variety of Creation. Now we have a self-sufficient art, in which second-hand matter is emptied out or denied; and it is argued that less is more. And what is strange is that less actually does appear to be more, because of the 'self-sufficiency' of the work, and, by extension, of the artist. But this gain in status actually disguises a loss in territory. There is, literally, less in the paintings. Again I do not want to be misunderstood. There are many 'empty' paintings for which one can have much respect as works of art: I have stood in front of Malevich's white paintings, Ad Rheinardt's black paintings, Agnes Martin's beautiful squares, enjoying the sense of a human ponder - ing the worlds of simple forms. But, this is not *the* world; and as there is a great deal less received, there is also much less given.

This issue is beyond representation. It is beyond a 'non-objective art' which is trying to be like music. Music may still be 'about' life, emotion, the real world, without being in any way programmatic, and an abstract art can at least attempt to equate to that. But what this new art is about is creating something self-sufficient which, if it has meaning and character, has first-order meaning given by the artist, rather than second-order derivative character. It is, in other words, at the exact opposite pole to that saying of Constable's:

> It appears to me that pictures have been over-valued; held up by blind admiration as ideal things, and almost as standards by which nature is to be judged rather than the reverse . . . Yet, in reality, what are the most sublime productions of the pencil [i.e. fine brush] but selections of some of the forms of nature, and copies of a few of her evanescent effects.[44]

We need to hear what we think we are seeing, the new relationship between artist and nature, confirmed by the historian. George Heard Hamilton succinctly defines the new art:

> In relation to the actual world, the work of art is no longer a description or an illusion of that actuality, but rather is in and of itself its own reality, a real thing, subject to the laws of art rather than of nature, *imposing its own system of relations upon nature.*[45]

That latter phrase is particularly suggestive. I remember one of the first modern sculptures I had seen, a brightly painted welded steel construction by Anthony Caro which had been placed on the lawn of a Cambridge college. I had no idea then that Caro was destined to become the 'new world order' of sculpture, or that I would come to appreciate his work. All I could see was that it had no balance or harmony in its relationships, that neither in colour or form did it relate to its surroundings, nor did its girder-sections have any relation to building or engineering. Whatever logic it had was certainly unearthly; it had landed like some alien thing

---

[44] *Discourses*, p. 68.
[45] *Painting and Sculpture in Europe*, p. 15, my italics.

from elsewhere; and yet there it stood, day after day, 'imposing its own system of relations upon nature'. It was indeed like an 'alternative reality'. (Later, when I saw more of Caro's work, it seemed to me that its formal wrong-footedness actually conveyed, in a humane way, some of the oddness of modern being in the world. But that also begs the question of whether 'modern being' is itself out of step with the way things are.)

The work of art, then, is now 'a real thing, subject to the laws of art rather than of nature'. It is its own world, with its own rules. This then is the summit of creativity, to have created something outside this Creation. I am sure we are taking Hamilton's words further than he intended, but within the framework we have discussed, such an admission is significant. A place with its own rules is its own kingdom. This is, in a sense, nothing new. People do make up their own rules. What is different here is that the work of art becomes an actual place, a spot of ground, as it were, where the writ of God does not run. In other words, with such works we move from the sense of subjective 'freedom' (from God), to a notional *place* of objective 'freedom'. Outside this Creation is a place where God is not. A place, or thing, that makes you believe God does not have ultimate authority is plainly an idol.

We have perhaps already accepted the logic of this. God is a problem to people. He knows too much. There is something in us that would much rather that God was not there; or that there was a place where he could be got away from. All the places on this planet have been looked at. But art? Can we put our spacecraft in art? Can we mentally get ourselves into a space where God is not, and make that a counterweight to the responsibilities and laws which impinge on us in 'the world out there'? It must seem improbable that so much could happen in the corner of a Cubist painting, or while adjusting our sense of gravity in the new world of a Caro, or while trying to press through into the subterranean spaces of a Rothko; but the logic is that once we are out of this creation, with evidence in every daisy and leaf of a personal God, we are our own masters. There are no doubt many versions of this, religious versions and atheist versions; but the conclusion of all of them is that 'I and thou', as Martin Buber called 'otherness', seen in love, has ceased to exist. [46] You might feel 'one with the universe', but you (and the universe) are on your own.

Pure creation – the Tate Gallery 'Bricks'

There is one further ramification of the theme. This is not so much the creation of alternative universes, as the concept of such pure creation that

---

[46] The great Jewish philosopher and theologian's *I and Thou* was published as *Ich und Du* in 1923, introducing the influential distinction between instrumental relationships (I-it) and the ideal mutuality of 'I-thou'. 'Thou' is the intimate form of address which the English language has lost.

it is completely independent. This might be said to put man in the place of God. Whether it has idolatrous power one must judge for oneself.

The example I am going to take is a work which at one time was notorious in Britain, *Equivalent VIII* (1966), the arrangement of firebricks purchased by the Tate gallery from the American sculptor, Carl André. No one who has heard André speak, or who has seen his other floor-sculptures, can doubt his sincerity or intelligence, nor that he has succeeded in opening up a vein of experience with a distinct power. The two layers of bricks succeed perfectly in the objective which we have seen described as the goal of modern art, to create something with 'its own reality'. This would appear to be its sole purpose. Clearly the bricks are not intended to be seen as bricks. Bricks on the floor of a gallery would have some quite different meaning or function, such as something left behind by builders. Nor are these bricks designed to give any experience of bricks that would enhance other brick experiences, like looking at walls. That would be back to second-order creation. These bricks have been de-bricked to become a work of art, which truly stands alone, neither brick, in their meaning, nor representing anything else. It is a true new creation. This is, one must admit, a considerable conceptual achieve - ment. And yet – it does not give anything. It succeeds in isolating the artist, and all who identify with him, as a pure creator; and it could, perhaps, function unconsciously as an idol, representing quasi–divine power. But like so many idols, its appearance is, to say the least, disappointing. There is nothing there. Because it has deliberately cut itself off from second-order creation, the reference to something beyond itself, there is no flow out from it, only a flow inwards. Instead of enriching life, it draws in life. Contrast this with the old Dutch backyard painted by De Hooch, which ennobles every brick for those who have seen it. Admittedly Carl André was not trying to do this, so it is unfair to compare; but it is also true that he has been publicly elevated to the De Hooch level, through pursuing his conception of artistic originality; though he has not first been, unlike De Hooch, a public servant. And when you think of what his pure creativity has actually produced, it is, compared to what a man might make, nugatory, a trifling offering. But this is, nonetheless, the true art of our times. Its well-springs are genuine, its public place is deserved: unless someone is going to start making choices.

See Plate 27 *(margin note)*

The effect on naturalistic art

This kind of art is not the whole of modern art; also, it may be thought that a minority of works was being taken too seriously. But even if individual works are avoidable, part of the strange power of them is the effect they have on everything else. For the 'serious artist', such arts as flower painting, landscape painting, paintings of animals, children, even portraits, are often to be regarded as somehow trivial, predictable, or second-best. The canvas of nature can come to seem too familiar, with nothing to say to us, whereas a nearly blank canvas in art, by contrast, can appear to embody dense wisdom.

One can understand that this art of new realities only got going because the heart had already gone out of the painting of the figure and of nature; we have seen that scientific rationalism had left the meaning and value of nature undefended. But nonetheless the new art has had its own vigorous effect, not acting in any way as a healer of these epistemological problems, but more effecting a curse over the older art, afflicting it with a sense of inferiority, redundancy or ineffectuality. It has been as if the life was continually sucked out of naturalism and its cognate styles into the vortex of the new negativity. One can readily experience this result in a gallery, where any attempt to look at naturalistic art after a period of immersion in the new art will make the older art look disengaged and light-weight, or as people say so easily, 'irrelevant and boring'; and locked into a time-frame which is of no concern to the present. Heaven help the present when it has only the present for its teacher.

But it was never true that naturalism had stopped working. There are the wonderful Neo-impressionist works of Gilman, painted during the Cubist years, as well as the stronger works of his French contem - poraries Vuillard and Bonnard. Gwen John is another great painter from this period. David Bomberg abandoned abstraction during his stay in Jerusalem, and painted roof-scapes of electric detail. The succession of these painters has never ended, and continues, to some extent, with Freud and Hockney in the present day. But the curse lingers, and the curse is that of having been sidelined. From the point of view of art, there is little to fault in these artists' works; but from the point of view of art history, they are at fault. They have missed the point. They could have strode tall, leading the public like philosopher kings, but instead they took the low road of the humble task, faithfully performed. They allowed themselves to be subject to the common view, the shared appreciation of the world which made them partners, not monopolists, in perception. They had no urge to become 'the acknowledged legis - lator of our spiritual, even of our political, condition', perhaps because they were intuitively satisfied with the laws we already have. Naturalism, showing people what is there, is in every generation too radical to command instinctive support. It requires not communing with the spirit of the age, but freedom.

See Plate 25

The idol of the artist

There is one further in this gallery of idols around the new art, that of the artist himself as the one who 'knows'. This idol does damage not so much to art as to people. It feeds on the guilt that the educated public bears towards the misunderstood and persecuted artist, and supplies in return the religious pleasures of hero worship. To read some of the art press, you would imagine that to speak with artists was to stand on holy ground. The highest form of human attainment, some writers imply, is to be the true worshipper and to understand the artist; in fact, since that gift of interpretation is so rare, it is slightly higher a manifestation of goodness than the compromised and grubby business of doing art itself.

We should not underestimate the difficulties of getting on the right footing with the artist, whose work we may not easily understand and whom we do not wish to subject too rashly to our own prejudices, and there is no harm in listening to their utterances with careful respect. But what is so damaging, to artists and to everyone else, is the submissiveness that regards the artist as having, in himself, irrespective of any ability to express it, a private and superior access to the truth. Any criticism therefore must represent a failure in understanding on our part. As a result there are probably too many half-understood and half-appreciated works being exhibited, because those empowered to take decisions about them have disempowered themselves, by sacrificing their judgement to the artist. They will not of course appear disempowered. They will shout loud approval as if it is their opinion that they are giving. But inwardly they will know that they are giving the artist the benefit of the doubt, because it is a matter of belief with them that the artist is the only valid authority. The artist is the one who 'knows', who alone understands the world. If, of course, the artist really believes that about himself or herself, that blasts into irrelevance the opinions of everyone else. This idol habitually destroys everything in its path. But those who fall in front of the juggernaut seem to like being trodden on.

The best art, however, does not leave you with the artist as its theme, but has the capacity to free you the better to be yourself. It makes connections, it stimulates you to paint or sculpt, it takes you by the hand as senior partner into a world that is really there. And it is full of pleasure, because life has taken hold of it, and it has found itself giving something back. This kind of art may suffer from epistemological oppression and every other disease of the age, but it is hard to suppress, because it has a life that is implicit in the craft. Though the way of idols is ever appealing, because it draws in powerfully, it is not fecund; its progeny are poorer than itself. The way of what we have called 'small art' may be less appealing because it bows itself under circumstance, time and place; it is a receptive art rather than one absolutely under the artist's control; but in that agreement to be a participator, rather than a ruler in life, the work of the 'small artist' is enduringly fruitful. Think of the good done by artists who have seen the world and opened horizons; and think of the trail of empty lives and distended egos produced by those who have mocked and closed doors.

Paganism, direct and diffuse

One more subject has to be mentioned in the context of live, practical idols, and that is paganism. There are people today who call themselves pagans, and who are trying to recreate pre-Christian religion, presumably in a sanitized, liberal form, so that they can live with their post-Christian consciences. Perhaps after this new movement has been around long enough, adherents will see enough of the social and ethical fall-out of not believing that humans were made in the image of God, who 'so loved the world, that he sent his only Son, that all that believe in him should not perish, but have everlasting life', that they will come to understand why pagans turned to Christianity in the first place. But the ground has been prepared for such a descent into naïveté, by several generations of artists who have tried for themselves to summon up the drumbeat of the earth religions, either consciously or by a sense of attraction and fascina - tion. Much just criticism has been levelled at Christianity having itself become too implicated in post-Enlightenment rationalism, so that 'Christ', to people of feeling and imagination, left them cold, a feature which the worldwide Pentecostal movement (in its broadest sense) of Christianity has begun to remedy. But ultimately the religion of earth and the faith of the Son of God cannot be combined. We should not look on the new paganism in art as merely reactive, or completely exonerate artists and others who are looking in the wrong direction for integration. This path is a path that is chosen, one that displays its own evidence, and which throws up its own, contentious, images.

Abstract Expressionism

It has become such a familiar feature of artistic biography that one hardly notices reading about the absorption into art of primitive imagery. Here is the early Pollock, producing authoritative, but violently confused images of semi-abstract, interlocking bodies:

> One can discern the strands in the melange but not unravel them: Picasso's bestial hybrids, ritual events from the allegories of the Mexicans and perhaps an even stranger dramaturgy drawing upon Native Amerindian legends. They surely also merged in Pollock's own mind, part of the tumult . . . Not surprisingly, a personal crack-up ensued . . . [47]

Or, from the same source, a section on the way in which totemic imagery, under the influence of Surrealism, seemed to have a particular relevance as a symbol for the dark powers released by the War:

---

[47] David Anfam, *Abstract Impressionism*, p. 75.

The Abstract Expressionists also rediscovered the authentically primi -
tivist vision of the totem as a hybrid between an animate presence and
a sign, sometimes geometric or schematic in character, yet still em -
bodying potent forces. To the Northwest Coast Indian, . . . [Barnett]
Newman wrote . . . a shape was a living thing, a vehicle for an abstract
thought-complex, a carrier of the awesome feelings he felt before the
terror of the unknowable . . . [it was] therefore, real . . . [The studio
of Clyfford Still] was once described as having 'totems and strange
images, both two- and three-dimensional, all around' . . . Images that
return our gaze, sculpture that broods and bristles with hostility . . .
had a special message in the years when malignant forces menaced
humanity.[48]

Instances could be multiplied. We normally absorb such information
complacently because of the undoubted power that primitive imagery has
brought to art.

We must not confuse two issues. The artistic power of primitive art
is often great, in that some of its practitioners have been masters of
expressive form; what they say, they say so well that it communicates
across the cultures and centuries. But what those twentieth-century artists
who have absorbed so much from them have been after is not formal
power in itself, but the expression of those things which primitive art was
trying to express. The psychologist Jung had paved the way for this by
his theory of myths and archetypes, by which he argued that there is a
substratum of universal beliefs, accessible through the imagery of different
religions or the unconscious. This step effectively left Christianity as a
local superstructure on a universal (pagan) substructure, rather than
paganism as a set of essentially local beliefs one could choose to hold, and
Christianity as the true universal. His view has so passed into the
consciousness of the art community that dipping one's bucket into the
wells of pre-Christian religion is seen now as a rational and meritorious
activity. The possibility that such a practice might be immoral in itself
does not usually enter our heads.

But take the idea of totemic images, 'sculpture that broods and bristles
with hostility', as an image for the malignant forces of war. It is true that
deeply occult power must have been behind both the Nazis' evil, and
their temporary success, and likewise behind the emperor worship that
drove Japan to its evil and suicidal war. Doubtless atavistic powers of a
destructive nature were also released in the armies of the allies. The
problem with primitivistic imagery for evil, however, is its lack of
discrimination. It is just as likely to summon it up as to identify it for what
it is. Of its nature, the imagery does not take sides. Or rather it is more
likely, unwittingly, to speak on behalf of evil, by acting to terrify, ('bristles

---

[48] Ibid., pp. 95–96.

with hostility'), than it is to exorcize it. Primitive religion deals with evil powers by a ritual of appeasement and accommodation, not by conquest. The result is that using such images indiscriminately as symbols for the forces of war, far from naming evil for what it is, produces an inability to distinguish between the powers of disruption and the powers of justice. Such an art may have the appearance of wisdom, in its power to expound evil; but in its inability to expose it, to take sides, it could be, unwittingly, immoral.

Henry Moore

More of a 'peacetime paganism' is evinced in the work of the British sculptor Henry Moore. The theme here is of the human and the natural as one continuum; George Heard Hamilton describes some of Moore's large figure sculptures as 'like totems of a forgotten faith'. Note how congenial religious language is to the art historian, as Hamilton continues:

> In his desire to assert the basic dignity and durability of human life as natural form, as form in nature, Moore may be considered a religious artist, or at least a philosophical one. But in a secular age which can no longer comprehend cosmological truths in figural terms, he has had to create his own mysteries, as well as his own icons. [49]

In other words, inventing your own religion, or 'mysteries', for the sake of artistic profundity is a permissible, even a benign purpose in a secular age. Hamilton has listed the main ingredients of Moore's development with the usual detachment of the art historian: 'African wood-carving, Assyrian reliefs, Etruscan tomb figures, archaic Greek sculpture, and ancient American art', and of course, the landscape itself. But while willing to discuss the quality of the work resulting, we, along with the historians, are normally very slow to question its spiritual meaning. But in a discussion of idolatry this is something we must do.

One could never assess the public, religious influence of Henry Moore's sculpture, displayed as it is in so many prominent places through - out the world. Some would undoubtedly view it humanistically, saying that an art that simultaneously promoted respect for the human body, especially the female body, and the landscape, cannot but be socially beneficial. Also an art of such obvious quality in its meditation on form and materials must also encourage opposition to the instant and shoddy in art, and perhaps foster a capacity to slow down and meditate in life. In all this there is an acceptable public face to Moore's work, that takes us very far from any suspicion of false religion. However, it is a similar merging between the human and the natural that is also the respectable

---

[49] Hamilton, *Painting and Sculpture in Europe*, p. 519.

public face of modern paganism, (at least of the ecological variety), on the simplistic understanding that the merging of their identities will be good for both. Are there observable negatives in Moore's treatment? Perhaps it is an obvious point, but the cost of the unifying of human and nature is the loss of the person. We have grown so accustomed to the pin-hole eyes of the primitive mask that we scarcely notice the blank eyes and tiny heads of Moore's figures, indicating the evacuation of the person from the human form. This has more than token religious implications. The person is accountable; the cherished landscape of eroded rock, however animated by some imaginary inner soul, is not.

Moore's work, occupying the public square in so many countries, has also taken on different meanings, its solid, homey qualities, rounded and well-made like the prow of a tanker, making it a permanent representative British export, so its religious beckonings are easy to bypass. But before we allow it to become a fixed part of our own art-historical firmament, we should recognize that if Moore has commitments in respect of the nature of the human, so have we, and that if ours are Christian, we cannot accept his without compromise. I know that this may seem disrespectful, but an experiment I like to try is mentally puncturing his work. Its vaunted weight, which can be so beguiling, the impressive sea-channelled hollows which draw you into its prehistoric mystery when earth and maternity and birth and fecundity were one, all can become instantly skin-thin, hollow exercises in bombast.

It is not nice to say that, and I do not say that that is what the works actually are, in their undoubted sculptural finesse; but seeing this way is the result of having made choices. To keep these works 'alive', to think of them as living things, I have had to breathe into them the breath of neo-pagan belief. This is none other than being lured into spiritual compromise by artistic sentiment. Better for me to allow them to deflate; and to regard the achievement of Moore as a religious and philosophical experiment that failed.[50]

★ ★ ★

The paganism of modern art, then, is not the serious paganism of today, with committees, posters, headed notepaper, and so forth, but for all we know it may have had considerably more influence in reinvoking the pagan powers. The works of art that have resulted from such deep drinking at the wells of primitive culture, by recent European and American artists, have had all the power, the ghostly, otherworldly power,

---

[50] A Christian writer who sees Moore's sculpture in an altogether different light, finding in it a wholesome depiction of motherhood, is Calvin Seerveld, in *Rainbows for the Fallen World*, p. 231: 'Henry Moore's life work is a moving corrective to the treatment of woman as a sex goddess or as a bagatelle, and deserves the attention of Christians looking for an alternative vision'.

that their makers sought. They would not of course have called their spiritually-suggestive works 'idols'. 'Idol' is the name given by those whose faith is committed already, to the God of Abraham, Isaac and Jacob. But because those works have the ability to attach the mind to old and new religious beliefs, I see no reason to withhold that word. If 'idol' seems an unduly hostile term, at least it is a reminder that art is a serious business.

Chapter Ten

The Invincible Qualities of Art

God's covenant with artists?

We could not leave this part without reminding ourselves, however, that the story of the slide of art into false religions and idolatry is only part of a greater story. One aspect of this greater story is the perceptible continuity of God's faithfulness to (underwriting of) art. This is not a theological add-on; it is a quite tangible fact of art as it comes to us.

The best way of understanding this is through the biblical account that the existence and good working of the Creation, of which art is a small part, is something that has been freely and deliberately prolonged by God, when it need not have been, in the face of its gross evil. Put another way, human evil is not the 'big story' in heaven, in the way it is in the earth's newspapers; it is not evil that is the surprise there. The 'big story' is God's mercy to his creation; his patience with it all, and redemption, are the news. This is most readily summarized in the promise of God to a very nervous Noah, as the earth was drying from the Flood:

> I will never again curse the ground because of man, for the imagination of man's heart is evil from his youth; neither will I ever again destroy every living creature as I have done. While the earth remains, seedtime and harvest, cold and heat, summer and winter, day and night, shall not cease. (Genesis 8:21–22, RSV)

For would-be demigods and tyrants, this graciousness of God has been very useful; they have been able to rely on the regular capacities of night and day, summer and winter for their schemes, even supplies of food, and have been given a quite illusory sense of their own strength. The willing functionality of Creation is something that is almost universally taken for granted. Taking it for granted deprives us of a lot of pleasure and wonder in seeing creation work, and also leaves us missing the sense of sheltering care which God intended, as a background to all the irregularities of life. In the sphere of art, subject though it is in the foreground to such serious abuse, there is also evident something of this *background covenant* with Creation.

God's 'covenant' through form and matter

It is well-known that science 'works'; this is a gift of Creation. But so also does art. Art, though subject to far greater stresses than science, cannot be pushed too far beyond itself. There seems to be something intrinsically truth-dealing and good in the interplay between man and materials. That, no doubt, is why there is frequently the cuckoo of idolatry in the nest; but the nest has been made, and made good, to begin with. The process itself is healthy, which is why we encourage children so much in art. Once matter and form are engaged with, it is inevitable that questions of relationship arise, and before long the person involved has humbled herself to enjoy organizing and ordering the things that are.

The capacities of art are capacities that the Creation inherently supplies. This fact supplies a consistent note of grace (a theological term, but the only possible word for the sense of the unlooked-for goodness of God, that is simply there) in the art gallery. Many have been the viewers who have been shocked by the content of Francis Bacon's work, but who have thoroughly enjoyed his skilled handling of paint. It is Bacon who has done that, but it is also the paint that he has responded to. Some artists have said they feel 'guilty' that they enjoy oil paint so much, or feel bad that it does so much for them. This is grace, which is troubling them; when the medium meets the artist half-way, and encourages them on, through no effort of their own.

The 'covenant with art' signifies that even the most devious idolater cannot avoid being about the business of art, once he is involved with art. That is why many 'primitive' cultures have succeeded in producing art under conditions that were not very propitious, considering the weight of tradition, the functionalism of images, and the lack of personal freedom. They have got involved with materials and form, and have taken off. Art can be about its business, even when religion fails it. Therefore we too can be about the business of enjoying art, form, expression, even when we need to positively dis-align ourselves with what it is trying to say. God has given a gift which is very difficult to destroy.

The unbreakable subject-object tie

Another aspect of art that works is the way it is useful for perception. As a metaphorical system, art has been tested to destruction, but it is very difficult for any image *not* to convey something. This is because the artist is working with two sorts of externality, the matter (medium) outside himself that he alters, or selects, and the world that is external to that. Some kinds of comparison cannot other than be made by us, and yield some degree of meaning. For example, one artist known for fairly minimal statements is the Italian, Lucio Fontana, the specialist in slashed canvases. The subject of such pictures is apparently 'a symbolic and physical escape

from the usual flat surface . . . In allowing us to look through the canvas
the artist creates another dimension and conveys a sense of infinity.' [51]

We would not necessarily guess this without someone to explain it
for us, but it is difficult, so great is the power of metaphor, to avoid
putting together some idea of meaning from the work. The human
mark, because it is human, has to be interpreted. And so great is the
perceptual optimism implanted in us, that we may even find his canvases
beautiful.

Therefore with all that we have said about subject–object tension, and
the conviction in philosophy departments that perception is a very
hazardous process, it remains true that the ability to relate to the world
out there, and to communicate what we think we understand, has been
almost laughably durable considering the strains that art has put upon it.
One would think that in times of epistemological doubt, extra care would
be taken by artists to make their meaning plain, but the reverse has been
the case. But even those artists who seem to make it as hard as possible
to understand their work succeed in conveying something of their
thoughts, life and times.

The credit for this state of affairs should be given, then, to something
indestructible about the structures of Creation. Put everything in cipher,
and your cry will still be heard. We should not be surprised. Even dumb
beasts can hardly fail to communicate what they want.

The mercy of meaning

It is supposed to be a problem that meaning is so variable. But this may
also be an aspect of the beneficent structures of Creation. It might seem
frustrating that every trip to an art museum is different, because works of
art evoke different meanings at different times, but it would be far more
so if every visit was identical. If a work of art could be processed by us
like a piece of information, such as 'that building is thirty metres tall', it
would never have to be looked at again.

Jesus was a student of variable meanings. The widow who gave such
a negligible sum in terms of the temple finances was seen by him as giving
a fortune. The same facts could be seen by anyone; the interpretation was,
if you like, highly 'subjective', but it was at the same time authoritative,
a claim about the actual truth (Luke 21:3). Poetry and art depend on such
transparencies, facets and levels of meaning. Another example might be
a child's drawing of multiple killings and explosions. What is the true
subject of the picture? Only the most gloomily pacifist parent would make
the mistake of taking it too literally. Perhaps it is some kind of love
offering, done with humorous delight, to the parent herself. The true
response to the 'meaning' is not anxiety, but enthusiasm.

---

[51] *The Art Book*, p. 159.

Therefore when we are looking at works of art, there are many levels on which their meaning can be enjoyed. We do not always have to be the grand inquisitor, looking for theological deviation. The real story of the work might be its show of artistic freedom, even when the mind of the artist was evidently constrained by what seem to have been false beliefs. It does us no harm to remember that it is God who judges, and he sees much going on in art, as well as life, apart from what we see. So we are wise to hold our judgements in an open hand.

Art, then, may not communicate tightly, but if it did, it would probably not be art, something that participates in the capacity of creation to enjoy the looseness, variability and freedom of its meanings; meanings which seem at times to buzz all over the place like quantum particles, but find their immediate purpose, and their ultimate resting place, in the dynamic providence of God. We cannot pin anything down and say 'this means that'. The most solemn existential investigation in paint may reappear as a next year's dress design. But this is what it is to live in God's world where redemption is at work, where we cannot control interpre - tations, and where God exercises authorial rights over everything we do.

Conclusion: there could be more

In view of all we have just been saying, it is difficult, even if it is desirable, to find a stable place from which to assess modern art. The idol may be there, if you want to use it; but there may be, indeed there certainly will be, other things happening at the same time. 'To the pure all things are pure', as St Paul wrote to Titus. But we are not all as pure as St Paul, and must remember our own suggestibility.

A more positive way of looking at modern art is that taken by many contemporary Christian artists, who are less concerned to judge it, than to see what they can do with it. They will be looking not just at the idolatry story, but also at the authenticity story, and the freedom story. They will be wanting to rephrase its meaning for new ends, rather as Gothic absorbed the Islamic arch so completely that its origin was forgotten. We cannot deny or reverse art history, or have any idea how it could be otherwise. But we can trust the Lord of history to do something with it, something unmistakably his. We can also look on the amazingly prolific and inventive art of our times, and see in it the creativity of God, even as he has allowed it the experiment of denying him.

The freedom of modern art is in large part the exploration of the freedom that God has given. This good freedom is also a freedom to sin. Constituted as we are, we prefer to find out the boundaries, rather than take them on trust. There must come a point, however, when we should admit to having found out what we think we need to know. The great experiment may have given a genuine art; but better still would be a genuine art that finds its way again to the centre. There is a way of occupying the centre with integrity, and that will be the theme of the final part.

PART IV

HOPE IN ART

There is a largely undiscussed assumption that the job of art is to fill out a century with a 'direction' and with progressive, revolutionary, develop - ments. I doubt if I am alone, at the end of the twentieth century, in finding the continuation of this view a depressing prospect. Do we always have to be looking forward to 'the future'? Today we are living in yesterday's future, and still we are supposed to be looking forwards. What about now?

And yet there is a drive forwards, but one which does not deny the present. It is that future, which gives the present meaning. It is that future which will spread out all our 'presents', like so many works of art, and look at them, and evaluate them , within the purposes of history as a whole.

This is the point in the book when I am most at risk of losing some of my readers. That is not, I hope, because the usual courtesies will not continue. It is because it is the part of the book most difficult to understand from outside the Christian story. Most of what we have seen so far has been based on the physical evidence of works of art, which has raised questions demanding answers. That has helped us stay on common ground. Here, however, we are beginning to speak of a hope for art, of which the evidence is largely internal.

I cannot easily see a way round this, except by keeping the discussion brief (it is brief too, because this is a huge subject, and we have gone far enough). To be sure, there is plenty of external evidence, of which I have illustrated some examples, of where I can see some (Holy) spiritual inflow into the art of the present. But I have to admit that you may not see what I see. There is the awkward species of experience called 'faith' to be taken into account. So I am taking the risk of asking you to take a deep breath, and try to imagine what an *insider's* view is like.

One final point. Mention the word 'faith', and some people will immediately begin to picture it as a kind of rather pleasant bubble, that some other people move around in, and just 'happen' to have, which insulates them from the 'normal' life that is going on around them. Perhaps we have got far enough in this book already to have made it clear that any faith we speak of is not of that kind. It is a quite realistic, urgent, belief that certain things have happened; and that certain things are going to happen. It is this future, not the unknown, but the expected, that gives the present condition of art its more than temporary importance.

Chapter Eleven

The Unfinished Story

This would be a chapter full of blank space, if the publishers could afford it. Shall we try some?

This is not so that we can bury our heads in white and meditate. It is to give the idea of a creative space, which is there to be filled, and which can be filled. There is nothing to fear for the future of art. The creative fountain has not run dry. Something in history has happened to make neither this time, nor any other time, the end of the line for art.

This has nothing to do with prediction. Prediction leads to despera -
tion. Art has suffered many 'near death' experiences this century, when
it has seemed that nothing further could be done, and all that was left was
a vision of whiteness. Or perhaps one might have experienced that
oppressive sense of walking along the art school corridor, looking at the
endless regurgitations of the art of the past, and thinking there is no 'future'
for art. But there is an energy which has nothing to do with prediction
of the future, more akin to 'trust'.

This is not to do with a trust in civilization. Much energy has come
into art and culture from a recycling of the art of the past. The work and
thought that took many unknown people many millennia to develop,
like some fossil fuel, can and has been introduced into our more hurried
age, transferring some of its own careful thought into it. But one wonders
how much longer that can go on: at each application, the transfer of
energy seems to get thinner and lighter. And global, mass-market culture
seems to have a unique ability to destroy, by trivialization, what it touches.
If this planetary civilization should run its course, it is hard to see where
it could be renewed from; except by an energy from the outside. But
suppose that energy from the outside (not a space-man energy, but
something more familiar, yet more powerful than that) is already here.

There is a parallel to the unknown horizon of culture, in the very act, the
common act, of creativity. When presented with a blank canvas, or a
blank page, there is no real reason why we should have any confidence
in the supply of the unknown to fill it. There is simply a boundary, the
edge of the space, and the possibly anxious thought that there really may
not be anything from outside it to fill it. Of course one can always copy
something. But what one wants is real life within the boundary. That has
got to come from somewhere – but since it is life, it does not exactly
come from within. When it happens, we accept it gratefully.

This sense of an undeserved supply may be taken as a sign that beyond
the boundary of existence itself, where we might fear there is nothing,
there is a life, completer and fuller (and more generous) than anything
we know here. This mystery of supply in creativity does not prove
anything, and there is plenty of creativity that goes wrong; but it is a sign
of that outside power, a power which one comes to believe in by other
means.

We perhaps do not need to remind ourselves, after all that has been said
in previous chapters, that it is not any old energy which one wants to
invite in from outside. There are bad energies as well, not divine but from
within the Creation; powerful, but not creative, only parasitic on crea -
tivity. The power that interests us is the power that really has life in it. I
know we customarily think of it as internal, though our forbears credited

it to 'the muses'. But the life we have perhaps developed a desire for in art is a life that even 'the muses' cannot generate. It harmonizes with us, but it is genuinely 'other': because it is the life of God.

How can this be real, within space-time? Do we have to think, like our pagan ancestors (and perhaps contemporaries), of a 'spirit world', which we hope is benign, sometimes acting on, and interacting with, this material world – two worlds, in a secretive, manipulative struggle for dominance? We would be unwise to: one of the pleasures, indeed necessities, of art and science in the Christian era is the realization that space-time is not the understudy for some activity going on elsewhere but is, as it were, the real performance, the real reality. So if any new energy is to have come in from the outside, it has to have really come into our existence as it is; not just filtered in as some internal perception for initiates.

What we are looking for, then, is something more than the sugges - tion that we can go forwards and backwards over the art of the past, drawing our strength from within the closed system. It cannot be denied that there is exciting creativity around, that seems to do just that. But the fact that art very often is supplied, seems to need to be translated into the assurance of supply; from outside, but also within space-time. We need a power-socket within finite reality, wired into the mains of an infinite supply.

I suppose we should all like it if Raphael had bequeathed to us his power of drawing; but we are talking here about something much greater than that, the means by which the spirit of life itself can in actuality become part of us.

You have arrived

You are emerging, you have been under water a bit too long and are gasping for air, and the sensation of looking upwards into light through splashes and swirls of blue water is still with you, as you try to shake the water from your eyes, and refocus. A group of friends gathers round you, and you hear applause. You have yourself done nothing, yet you are glad, and they seem as pleased as if something much more than a wetting has just happened to you. Now you are back on terra firma *with a towel. Someone pronounces that you have passed 'from death into life'. You were dead, now you are in life. Is this what has happened?*

The point of this illustration, which will not be obscure for long, is to suggest something highly physical, which is different from the more detached process of reading a book. A book can change one's perception, and that is valuable. But the kind of reception of life we are talking about has to be more than that; it has to be something that really happens to you, that indeed 'marks' you. Baptism, which I have just described, is the

best outward sign that could be devised. It is intended to symbolize a kind
of transplant operation, but one in which the patient dies!

This book will make more sense if this is appreciated, even if, heaven
forbid, this news frightens the reader into drawing back. We could of
course have written a book which was a market-stall of ideas, some of
which one might hope to pass on; we could have offered our story as a
coach tour of an ancient, quaint, apparently still surviving civilization.
Christianity and art is an interesting subject. But for some of us involved
in art, it cannot be just a subject 'out there', and Christianity is more than
a set of concepts. So we have to talk about something that must happen
outside a book. If there is anything valuable in the 'way of seeing' in the
book, of course one hopes some of it is transferable: but the real,
transformed way of seeing has to be to do with something that happens
inside a person, beyond anything to do with a book. When that has
happened, one does not need a book by which to see.

Is there an event, something we can know from history, that has really
happened, which can become a continuing event as we link up with it,
in which subjective and objective join?

The Crisis of history

When the Son of God exposed his body on this earth to be nailed to
death, one of them, his body or this earth, was going to crack.[52] He
allowed his body to crack; the earth was saved. That not just forgiven,
but mended earth has been the theatre of our existence from that time
onwards, and indeed from that time backwards.

By any justice, but the divine, in which God carried what was deserved
within himself, this mercy should not have happened. But the empty
tomb, and the resurrection life of Jesus, are more than mercy; they are
signs of a great wholeness in the forgiveness of God, by which individuals
can pass, from a state of uncertainty of their acceptance by him, or
certainty of their non-acceptance, to a condition of full reinstatement and
freedom.

Guilt is a terrible burden in the world. Conversely, forgiveness, and
the sense of unguilty connectedness with God, gives uprightness to a
person which is bound to affect their art. This can be seen in many ways,
and through many different manifestations of Christianity in history.
There is, I am sure, an overflow outside the confines of Christian faith,
so we are not trying to create a Christian 'brand'. We are merely trying
to notice some of the outward evidence in the art of Christians of 'what
has happened'.

---

[52] Colossians 1:17 states of Christ that 'in him all things hold together'. It is
dangerous, presumably, to attempt to pull the plug on 'the author of life' (Jesus,
as described by Peter in Acts 3:15).

What follows brings together comments about the effects for art of Jesus Christ throughout this book. There is, if you like, an outer side, the effect on the way the world is seen; and there is an inner side, the effect of Christ on the way individuals respond.

a) Reality nailed down

The first effect of what Christ has done is that reality has been 'nailed down', allowed fully to be itself, permitted to be what it really is, in contours and relief. This has been the launching ground for Western art.

The biggest complaints made to God, the God of the Bible, are about reality. The biggest complaints one hears about God, concern what he has or has not done about real life. This is not usually taken as a compliment to him. In 'mid-term', his government is hugely unpopular. The specialists and the faithful like him, but there are many people with grudges. Lift the lid on society, and there is a lot of noise about God going on.

But this is a compliment to God. We do not get this in Buddhism. With this God, the God of the Bible, we know one thing for sure even if we understand nothing else. What is happening to us, good or bad, really is happening. It is perfectly real. Sorting out why it is going on, that is the question.

In some societies you do not even complain. There is no one to complain to. When the judge comes, then people start to prepare their complaints. The story of art since Christ shows that now people are allowed to feel the pain of this life; because the judge has come, and he will (must, some feel, who do not even know him) sort it out.

We cannot, very fully, understand the work of the Cross. But we know it was not an operation under anaesthetic, putting the world into a deep sleep, from which everyone awakes, feeling much better. Many of us would like God to have done such an operation, curing us without knowledge or pain. But it was not so. Neither was it a secret work of smoothing and polishing, rubbing down rust and burnishing until every – thing gleams, and then we can admire the result. We would all like life to have been polished up and improved. But life has not been left gleaming. No, God's work was an operation which, far from planing and finishing, has soaked the wood and raised its grain so that every painful splinter can be seen and felt. Life has got more difficult since the Christians came along: it is seen more, felt more, tested more, exposed more. The heights are more, the depths are more; and even when the wells of culture drop deep into nihilism, anger and despair, they are Christian-dug wells, with buckets of Christian-taught anguish. The Old Testament character Job cried out for justice, in his horrific and 'unjust' suffering, because he knew God. Injustice is only fully felt where justice has been seen. Even atheism is a refusal of something known. The power to complain, to mock, to blaspheme God all results from God's exposure of himself through Jesus Christ. Indeed, blasphemy is the most consistent verbal witness to God; reality nailed down and felt, even when its whole meaning is not acknowledged.

I am visualizing the violence, and the tenderness of our art; and saying that, after Jesus died and was raised, it was not so easy to miss the truth. He has left a deposit which comes into almost everything we do.

b) Perception wired up

That was the outer truth, the plumb line that Jesus brought that showed how things were. But there is also the matter of inner truth. Inner truth requires action. If the connections are restored between outer and inner worlds, the inner person has to respond. That requires power.

I used to be bothered by the thought that something that happened two thousand years ago could hardly affect me now. This was quite unreasonable of me; after all, I never complained that penicillin was discovered a long time ago. But I had no idea that what was done was what I needed. I became less bothered when, as God came more into focus, that time distance collapsed, and still less bothered when I discov - ered that the 'event then' had been completed by something for now. 'You will receive power . . .', said Jesus (Acts 1:8).

See Plate 32

I am a little reluctant to say how this works for me in such art as I do myself, but I do not want to speak for anyone else. It is a great thing, to begin with, for God to have so restored connections to matter, so that one works with it sympathetically; and connections to people, so that one relates to them (they are a big part of the work) a little more as he does. But to know God's love in respect of art, so that one no longer has to compete, to be jealous, to be anxiously perfectionist or fearful of failure; that begins to put art in a wholly different place. It ceases to be a tyrant, or an enemy, and becomes something more of a friend.

In this new wiring, some of the horizontal connections are discon - nected; the pressures connecting you to fashion, to the esteem of others, to achieving a certain role. But the new connections that are made, vertically to God, and horizontally to the things that interest him, create a whole new sphere of life. You can enjoy the flowers of the field, just as Dürer enjoyed the hairs on his famous Rabbit, without the least sense that they are unimportant.

Recreated humans in history

It is one thing to speak of personal experience, which one hopes could be repeated from other accounts. But if what the Bible says is true, 'new life' is something we should expect to see in history.

Of course there is plenty of historical evidence of Christianity in art; icons, Church art, Christian subject-matter. But we are looking for something more personal than choice of subject-matter. 'If anyone is in

Christ, he is a new creation', the New Testament tells us (2 Corinthians 5:17), a phrase which does not mean a benign ecclesiastical compliment ('you are now a very nice person'), but a complete refashioning, in which the Creator of the universe has been involved. What have these new-style artists been doing?

The truth is, we have got almost too used to their work. To be sure, some have more about them of the new structure of understanding which came through Christ, than they share in his inner nature. Those artists who have had the particular sweetness of Christian temperament, the Giottos, the Fra Angelicos, are rare. But rugged Dürer, and calm Holbein, these are also men of faith, and Michelangelo could not have been Michelangelo without the Christian story, which eventually he made so much his own. Everywhere you look, there is faith, refracted in one degree or other through the flawed crystal of character and place.

Just to remind ourselves that these kinds of observation are the old commonplaces of art history, it may be worth quoting from a once much-printed book, Sir William Orpen's *Outline of Art*:

> The history of modern art begins with St Francis of Assisi, the most loveable of all the Christian saints. He, the first forerunner of the Renaissance, substituted a religion of love for the sterile authority of orthodoxy, and in his infinite charity brought divinity nearer not only to mankind but to all creation. The birds and the fishes are his little brothers and sisters, and like the Psalmist of old he calls the hills and the valleys, the rivers and the woods, to join him in praising God. In a word, by his teaching, religion was reconciled to nature, and with Nature again piously occupying the minds of men, art could progress. [53]

In the language we have been using, Orpen is talking about both a new 'structure' of the world being seen; that is to say, the realization that the background details of the world, mountains, streams, valleys, flora and fauna were in themselves significant and valuable; and new 'connections' being made with them, through love. It is astonishing how many of the Assisi stories of Francis are stories about places, so that the account given of them in the frescoes confirms what has already been sensed, that the Christian presence is very much to do with a job on the ground.

I would like to have talked about the outflow of these realizations down the centuries, right down to Cézanne, whose grateful respect for the Creator seems to have been one of the qualities that re-charged his passion. But this is something we need to do for ourselves, perhaps without an author as companion guide. It is possible to go into an art gallery with God, as a person, rather than as a trunkful of ideas.

---

[53] *Outline of Art*, p. 9.

Where are the miracles? (the Holy Spirit in art)

Some of the instances of the Holy Spirit's work in Old and New Testaments, not to mention reports coming in from all over the church today, were exceedingly dramatic. They were, and are, definite signs that a new regime is in charge and a new order under way. One would like to think that the same Holy Spirit had had some definite effects in art. Otherwise, has the Spirit been there at all?

I suppose we should ask ourselves what we expect. The habit of taking all kinds of creativity for granted causes us to miss a great deal of what the Holy Spirit does. But his work is neither nebulous nor inessential. We can see this from the classic Old Testament example of creativity.

The first mention of the Spirit anointing any individual (Exodus 31), is when two artists were being prepared for work. The anointing is clearly something that they need: and when one considers the work, one can understand why. They are being equipped for a prolonged period of inventive and skilled work with precious materials, for the preparation of a worship centre, which it is intended will speak in its own language about the being and presence of God. The work these artists need to do has to be authoritative; it must not distract from worship by being 'about them' as artists, rather than 'about God'. In order to do that it must be indeed 'in his Spirit'; it must come out of his overflow, rather than from theirs.

The artists must also get their work right artistically, and thus need equipping for physical and mental concentration. Even such decorative work must be done in a free and creative spirit rather than mechanically, so that as a whole, as in the part, it is all alive. Then there is the matter of invention. The ideas have got to come from somewhere. The team of artists, named Bezalel and Oholiab, no doubt already have well-stocked imaginations and long experience of design. But they are looking for fresh wisdom in combination and variation of what they know, and perhaps trusting that they will be given patterns and sequences that they have never thought of before. At that stage of beginning, they will have known very much the need for a power to come to them from the outside.

In *Voicing Creation's Praise*, the author speaks wisely of the Holy Spirit's work in art as to do with making connections. [54] This is a powerful, indeed indispensable activity, which is nonetheless powerful for being hidden. The Spirit links ideas, brings things to mind, but above all makes the *primary connection with truth* that brings our art really alive. We do not necessarily need what is novel: we need to be connected to that which is already there. The Holy Spirit is the creative partner in bringing things together.

---

[54] Jeremy Begbie, p. 226.

A complementary 'quiet work' of the Spirit relates to the meaning of his name in Hebrew, that of 'breath' (and wind). Our breathing puts the rhythm into the music we play, the words we write, and into our brush strokes. Breath, the pace and life of breathing, short and tense, slow and steady, deep and passionate, is the perceptible spirit of art; the 'person' we relate to in performance, book or painting. The Holy Spirit, the 'breath' of God, (I am convinced) puts his life in our rhythms, so that a Spirit-empowered work is in some way breathed with him. Together with the strength and wisdom of combination that he gives as the 'connector', this makes for the perceptible touch of God's Spirit in a work, (as opposed to merely man's spirit, or the world's spirit, or even a demonic spirit).

If we may use the Israelite tent (worship centre) to some extent as a model, the Spirit is present in the work of art in some sense as a *partner*. The work is not wholly his; to think so would be a pretence, which would hardly explain the need for artists to do the work. But he is the one who briefs, supplies, corrects, encourages and receives what the artist does; in fact, he is the ideal patron! Then there is the matter of *authority*. There is nothing he supplies to guarantee that any work of art has the authority of God; but there is something of his wisdom so imbuing a work that it can, quite justifiably, come to have an authority beyond anything the artist could have given it. It has a certain character that is beyond space-time to explain. But the work of art may be so humble that this quality will hardly be noticed. It is simply that there are now present, as additions to Creation, objects which seem perfectly 'right', to belong as if they ought always to have existed. Are these miracles, then?

I think these ordinary creative events should not be underrated. I am not thinking of just any art, or of the creative 'nothings' of art, clever though may be their conception. I am talking about the somethings, the medieval chalices with endlessly varied and wonderfully organized filigree ornament; the decoration of boss and capital in the Gothic cathedral, those places where there is something, when there could easily be nothing. Indeed there is wonderful decoration and art in every civilization: but I am talking of that fullness, a clarity and sharpness and generosity of beauty and imagination which perhaps particularly comes from God through Christ. But now I am wandering into proof, and we shall soon get into disputes.

It surely is a sort of miracle, and it does not happen all that frequently or easily, when something is produced that is really better than what was there before. Then that echoes and exemplifies the whole principle which Jesus came to show: that something altogether new and good can happen within our supposedly closed system.

Personal profile for the Christian artist

See
Plates
28–33
I know a few Christian artists, and they are all different. [55] Some paint
Bible themes, doing the impossible of rethinking new images for today,
and doing so with evident enjoyment; others paint nature, domestic
themes, or else enjoy abstraction. Sometimes a theme is polemical,
sometimes it is just an aspect of the world that the artist feels to be
important. It is like all the different ways of being human. But there may
be some common features on which they would agree.

I think a Christian artist would accept the *limitation of art*. Art is, though
unique and important, just one thing in the world. It does not control
the world, it does not convert people, it is not something that heals; if
you try to think of it instrumentally you are in for disillusionment. It really
only makes sense as something that is done 'unto God', rather than to
'do' anything; it is something that has to be done, as part of the totality
of truth, (and the fact that non-art solutions are so unsuited to this beautiful
world); and it is something that by some sort of economic mercy one is
occasionally allowed to do. Art is something that has to be done, because
you are human, but the only way to justify it, is when you realize that
God would be disappointed if it wasn't there.

I think a Christian would understand something about *dependence on
God in art*. It is very complicated, and a little knot-tying, trying to explain
how something is 'really God', and not yourself at all, especially when
you have been up half the night praying and preparing and making it
happen. But what you do mean is that when you try to do the same thing
without a sense of absolute dependence on God, for strength, ideas, for
the very life of the thing, it does not work at all. Now it is true that
someone else might be satisfied with it. But you have developed a taste
for work with the 'God element' in it; you begin to recognize it in your
own work, and feel extremely cross with yourself when it is not there.
There is something special that God, of his kindness, brings into a work,
where you can truly say: 'I could never have done that myself'. I hope
there is some of it in this book.

I think that a Christian would know that *art is not the only thing* in their
own personal life. This can be unnerving. Since it does not master us, we

---

[55] Two points about the illustrations (Plates 28–33): first, the selection is not to
be taken as 'representative', either of the artists' whole work or of Christian
painters in general. It is simply an informal gathering of works by a few painters
known to me: whose work I like. Second, the slight preponderance of Christian
subject matter is not to be taken as implying that that is all that Christians paint.
However, it does seem to have happened that, having been liberated from the
obligation to paint biblical themes by the teaching of e.g. Hans Rookmaaker
some years back, many artists have begun to find them extraordinarily interesting.

really do have to choose to do it. When the lust has gone, loyalty to God has to replace it.

Finally, it would be interesting to ask how the Christian artist felt about other artists. Would they encourage each other, though often so different in work, style, and aim, and would they pray for each other? In my experience, they would.

What about hope?

This is a big issue, and it is appropriate that it should come at the end of the book. Suzi Gablik, in her book, *The Reenchantment of Art*, makes the point that art needs hope, or it cannot survive. [56] She sees hope as in very short supply, and one of the purposes of her book is to restore a sense of hope. Some of the stories she tells of the humane things that some artists are doing do indeed provide a measure of comfort that the love and kindness has not completely gone out of the world. Perhaps her hope is that the nihilistic bottom of the pendulum-swing has been reached, and that humanity, now dissolving the 'Cartesian dualisms' that have fed the masculinely controlling (as she sees it) 'dominator culture', is once more on the up. There are periods in history when expectations are restored, and possibilities seem to flow again.

However one of the biblical writers remarks: 'hope that is seen is not hope' (Romans 8:24), and one can see why. To maintain this kind of hope one has to be very selective. Some new stories fit, others do not. As an American writer, Suzi Gablik knows that the prognosis of contempo - rary civilization, if you put current fears geo-political, social, and envi - ronmental together, is not all that good. And yet she rightly says that art needs hope.

★ ★ ★

Why does art need hope? Because art is, at its centre, creative, which means bringing to birth, by a kind of process of love, things that were never there before. These new things come into the environment of the world for their existence. And just as people do not easily want to bring children into the world in time of war, so art in a time of despair is in a hostile atmosphere. Love makes no sense. There is nothing to justify the freedom, the extravagance of time, the playfulness and the beauty of art. But art has to carry on as if love is true, the valid thing about the world. Art has the effrontery to be a song, when there are people dying. It does not make sense, but it is needed, and in some way, people know it is true.

The only way in which this can work, is not by consoling ourselves with the evidence that there is love and goodness in the world, but if love

---

[56] Gablik, p. 24ff.

actually is true. This is something that has to be true, whatever the evidence on the ground. Our art has to be supernaturally tuned, to a signal from outside. Which indeed it is, because that is art, and there is no other real art to be had.

But of course it is no good having a general belief in love: 'all you need is love', however true, and welcome to hear it said. Love is no good if it is out there and cannot touch in here. For love to actually be, in some sense, a global absolute, sufficient to sustain belief in art, it has to be more than an ideal. It would be useless having a big notice up in the sky saying 'love is the main thing'. All we would want to know is 'who put it there?', and more important, *'what is he going to do about it?'*

See Plate 33 Which is where the fact, unfortunately not much advertised, (and admittedly a faith-fact; you cannot buy a timetable) that Christ is due to return becomes very important. It has to happen that all the nonsense will be sorted out, and all the moral relativists and compromisers and deliberate cheats will have their surprise, and the thrones of lies and oppressions will be pulled down. When this happens, it will be apparent that hope in art was never like a cry for the past to return, or for the future to improve, but always more like a presentiment of what was going to take place, something to bank on, freeing up the conviction that an art of meaning could be sustained.

When we talk about an art of meaning, which is my shorthand for an art that is linked with external truth, but not necessarily the truth that we immediately see, because it includes the joy that will come when the pain is over, there is always the suspicion that we might be trying to talk ourselves into a new movement, a new cause. Such things, for all the value that campaigns sometimes have, are really human-based pro -grammes, limited and temporal. What we are really talking about is the freedom not to have to go along with the confinements of the present age, not through individualism, or the ability to get one step ahead, but because of a rootedness in the values of heaven. This is different from finding that the values implanted in creation appeal, though that is a start; it is more like an understanding that, radically strange as those values may sometimes seem, one day they will be vindicated; and if so, we are not so foolish to enjoy, and inhabit, that world of values now.

Bibliography

The following is a list of books mentioned in the text, and a few others that have been particularly helpful.

Anfam D., *Abstract Expressionism*, London: Thames and Hudson, 1990

The Art Book, London: Phaidon 1996

Augustine, *City of God*, Harmondsworth: Penguin, 1984

Bagley R.W., *The Times China Exhibition*, Souvenir Issue, 1996

Barzun J., 'The Rise of Art as Religion', in *The Use and Abuse of Art*, Mellon Lectures, 1973, Princeton Unversity Press, 1990

Begbie J., *Voicing Creation's Praise, Towards a Theology of the Arts*, Edinburgh: T & T Clark, 1991

Berger P.L., Berger B., and Kellner H., *The Homeless Mind*, Pelican Books, Harmondsworth: Penguin, 1974

Carson D.A., *The Gagging of God: Christianity Confronts Pluralism*, Leicester: Apollos, 1996

Chang Jung, *Wild Swans*, London: Flamingo, 1991

Chipp H.B. ed., *Theories of Modern Art, a source book by artists and critics*, London: University of California Press, 1968

Constable J., *Discourses*, edited by R.B. Beckett, Vol XIV, Suffolk Records Society, 1970

—, *Correspondence*, edited by R.B. Beckett, Vol VI *The Fishers*, Suffolk Records Society Vol XII, 1968

Cooper D., *The Cubist Epoch*, London: Phaidon, 1971

Cork R., *The Bitter Truth, Avant Garde Art and the Great War*, London: Yale and Barbican, 1994

Denton M., *Evolution: a Theory in Crisis*, London: Michael Joseph, 1978; revised edition, London: Burnett Books,1986

Fox R.L., *Pagans and Christians*, Harmondsworth: Penguin 1988

Fry R., *Vision and Design*, 1920

—, *Transformations*, 1927

Fuller P., *Theoria: Art, and the Absence of Grace*, London: Chatto and Windus, 1988

Gablik S., *The Reenchantment of Art*, New York and London: Thames and Hudson,1991

Gilot F. and Lake C., *Life with Picasso*, London: Thos. Nelson, 1965

Gombrich E.H., *Art and Illusion, a Study in the Psychology of Pictorial Representation*, London and Oxford: Phaidon Press, 1961

—, *Sense of Order*, London and Oxford: Phaidon Press, 1979

Gunton C., *The One The Three and the Many*, Cambridge: Cambridge University Press, 1993

Hamilton G.H., *19th and 20th Century Art*, New York: Abrams, n.d.

—, *Painting and Sculpture in Europe 1880–1940*, Pelican History of Art, Harmondsworth: Penguin, revised edition, 1972

Hardy D.W., and Ford D.F., *Praising and Knowing God*, Philadelphia: Westminster Press, 1985

Hibbard H., *Michelangelo*, Harmondsworth: Penguin, 1978

Mandelstam N., *Hope Against Hope*, Harmondsworth: Penguin, 1975

—, *Hope Abandoned*, Harmondsworth: Penguin, 1976

Middleton J.R. and Walsh B.J., *Truth is Stranger Than it Used to Be*, London: SPCK, 1995

Nash P., *Outline, a Fragment of an Autobiography*, Faber, 1949

Newbigin L. *The Gospel in a Pluralist Society*, London: SPCK, 1989

—, *Proper Confidence*, London: SPCK, 1995

—, *A Word in Season*, Edinburgh: St Andrews Press/Grand Rapids: Eerdmans, 1994

Orpen W.(ed.), *Outline of Art*, London: George Newnes, c. 1923

Polanyi M., *Personal Knowledge*, London: Routledge and Kegan Paul, 1958

Rewald J., *Cézanne Letters*, Oxford: Bruno Cassurer, 1976

Rookmaaker H. *Modern Art and the Death of a Culture*, 1970, reprinted Leicester: Apollos, 1994

Ryken L., *Work and Leisure*, Leicester: IVP, 1989

Scott D. *Everyman Revived, The Common Sense of Michael Polanyi*, Lewes, Sussex: The Book Guild Ltd, 1985

Scruton R., *The Aesthetics of Architecture*, London: Methuen, 1979

Seerveld C., *Rainbows for a Fallen World*, Toronto: Tuppence Press, 1980

Torrance T.F., *Theological Science*, Oxford: Oxford University Press, 1978

—, *Divine and Contingent Order*, Oxford: Oxford University Press, 1981

—, *The Ground and Grammar of Theology*, Belfast: Christian Journals Ltd, 1980

Turner, Tate Gallery, 1974

Unrau J., *Looking at Architecture with Ruskin*, London: Thames and Hudson, 1978

Vine W.E., *Dictionary of New Testament Words*, London, 1940

Walford J., *Ruisdael*, New Haven and London: Yale University Press, 1991

Watkin D., *Morality and Architecture*, Oxford: Oxford University Press, 1977

Wilson D., *Hans Holbein, Portrait of an Unknown Man*, London: Weidenfeld and Nicolson, 1996 (paperback edition, London: Phoenix, 1997)

Wolterstorff N., *Art in Action*, Grand Rapids, Michigan: Eerdmans, 1980
Wright N.T., *The Climax of the Covenant*, Edinburgh: T & T Clark, 1991
—, *Colossians*, Tyndale Commentary Series, Leicester: IVP, 1986
—, *Jesus and the Victory of God*, London: SPCK, 1996
—, *What Saint Paul Really Said*, Oxford: Lion, 1997

★ ★ ★

For art students:
A useful 'art pack', with a selection of articles, fuller reading list and copies of Hans Rookmaaker's *Art Needs No Justification*, and excellent essay by Derek Kidner, *The Christian and the Arts*, is available from UCCF, 38 De Montfort Street, Leicester, England, LE1 7GP, tel. 0116 2551700.

Index

This short Index is included to help you find, or go back to, some of the main points, not already listed in the Contents, of the discussion.

Made in the USA
Coppell, TX
27 February 2021